JAVASCRIPT BOOTCAMP

FROM ZERO TO HERO

HANDS-ON LEARNING FOR WEB DEVELOPERS

4 BOOKS IN 1

BOOK 1
JAVASCRIPT FUNDAMENTALS: A BEGINNER'S GUIDE TO WEB
DEVELOPMENT

BOOK 2
INTERMEDIATE JAVASCRIPT MASTERY: BUILDING WEB APPLICATIONS
WITH ES6 AND BEYOND

BOOK 3
ADVANCED JAVASCRIPT TECHNIQUES: MASTERING COMPLEX PROJECTS
AND FRAMEWORKS

BOOK 4
JAVASCRIPT NINJA: HARNESSING THE FULL POWER OF THE LANGUAGE

ROB BOTWRIGHT

Published by Rob Botwright
Library of Congress Cataloging-in-Publication Data
ISBN 978-1-83938-576-6
Cover design by Rizzo

Disclaimer

The contents of this book are based on extensive research and the best available historical sources. However, the author and publisher make no claims, promises, or guarantees about the accuracy, completeness, or adequacy of the information contained herein. The information in this book is provided on an "as is" basis, and the author and publisher disclaim any and all liability for any errors, omissions, or inaccuracies in the information or for any actions taken in reliance on such information.

The opinions and views expressed in this book are those of the author and do not necessarily reflect the official policy or position of any organization or individual mentioned in this book. Any reference to specific people, places, or events is intended only to provide historical context and is not intended to defame or malign any group, individual, or entity.

The information in this book is intended for educational and entertainment purposes only. It is not intended to be a substitute for professional advice or judgment. Readers are encouraged to conduct their own research and to seek professional advice where appropriate.

Every effort has been made to obtain necessary permissions and acknowledgments for all images and other copyrighted material used in this book. Any errors or omissions in this regard are unintentional, and the author and publisher will correct them in future editions.

TABLE OF CONTENTS - BOOK 1 - JAVASCRIPT FUNDAMENTALS: A BEGINNER'S GUIDE TO WEB DEVELOPMENT

TABLE OF CONTENTS - BOOK 2 - INTERMEDIATE JAVASCRIPT MASTERY: BUILDING WEB APPLICATIONS WITH ES6 AND BEYOND

TABLE OF CONTENTS - BOOK 3 - ADVANCED JAVASCRIPT TECHNIQUES: MASTERING COMPLEX PROJECTS AND FRAMEWORKS

TABLE OF CONTENTS - BOOK 4 - JAVASCRIPT NINJA: HARNESSING THE FULL POWER OF THE LANGUAGE

Introduction

Welcome to "JavaScript Bootcamp: From Zero to Hero - Hands-On Learning for Web Developers." In this comprehensive book bundle, we embark on an exciting journey into the dynamic world of JavaScript, the language that powers the web. Whether you're a novice aspiring to become a web developer or an experienced programmer looking to master JavaScript, this bundle is your key to unlocking the full potential of this versatile language.

"JavaScript Bootcamp: From Zero to Hero" is designed to take you on a progressive and hands-on learning adventure, starting with the foundational concepts and culminating in advanced mastery. The bundle consists of four carefully crafted books, each tailored to your skill level and aimed at equipping you with the knowledge and skills needed to excel in web development.

In "Book 1 - JavaScript Fundamentals: A Beginner's Guide to Web Development," we lay a solid groundwork for your journey. This book is your passport to the world of web development, introducing you to JavaScript's essential building blocks. You'll learn about variables, data types, control flow, functions, and how to work with arrays and objects. By the end of this book, you'll have a strong grasp of JavaScript fundamentals, setting the stage for your progression to the next level.

"Book 2 - Intermediate JavaScript Mastery: Building Web Applications with ES6 and Beyond" is your gateway to modern JavaScript development. We dive deeper into the language, exploring advanced topics such as ES6 features, asynchronous programming with Promises, DOM manipulation, and event handling. You'll gain the skills needed to create interactive and dynamic web applications, all while leveraging the latest JavaScript capabilities.

"Book 3 - Advanced JavaScript Techniques: Mastering Complex Projects and Frameworks" propels you into the realm of advanced web development. You'll tackle complex projects and dive into popular JavaScript frameworks like React, Angular, and Vue.js. With this knowledge, you'll be equipped to build scalable and maintainable applications, ready to face the challenges of the modern web development landscape.

"Book 4 - JavaScript Ninja: Harnessing the Full Power of the Language" is the pinnacle of your journey. Here, we explore advanced concepts such as functional programming, metaprogramming, concurrency, and memory management. You'll emerge as a JavaScript ninja, capable of solving even the most intricate development puzzles and creating custom JavaScript libraries tailored to your needs.

Throughout this bundle, you'll find hands-on examples, practical exercises, and real-world projects that reinforce your learning. We believe that the best way to master JavaScript is by doing, and each book provides you with ample opportunities to apply your newfound knowledge.

Whether you're a beginner taking your first steps in web development or an experienced coder seeking to elevate your JavaScript expertise, "JavaScript Bootcamp: From Zero to Hero" offers a guided path to success. With dedication and practice, you'll emerge from this journey as a web development hero, capable of creating remarkable web experiences and contributing to the ever-evolving digital landscape. So, let's embark on this adventure together and unlock the limitless possibilities of JavaScript.

BOOK 1
JAVASCRIPT FUNDAMENTALS
A BEGINNER'S GUIDE TO WEB DEVELOPMENT

ROB BOTWRIGHT

Chapter 1: Introduction to JavaScript

JavaScript is a dynamic, versatile programming language that has played a pivotal role in shaping the modern web. It was first introduced in 1995 by Netscape as a client-side scripting language for enhancing web pages. Over the years, JavaScript has evolved significantly, expanding its capabilities and becoming an integral part of web development. From its early days of simple interactivity, JavaScript has grown into a powerful language capable of handling complex tasks and running on both the client and server sides. This evolution has been driven by a thriving developer community, ongoing standardization efforts, and the need to keep pace with the ever-changing demands of the web.

One of the most significant milestones in JavaScript's history was its standardization under the name ECMAScript. ECMAScript is the formal specification for the JavaScript language, and it defines the syntax, semantics, and core features of the language. The first edition of ECMAScript was published in 1997, and subsequent editions have introduced new features and improvements to JavaScript. ECMAScript 6, also known as ES6 or ECMAScript 2015, was a major leap forward, bringing enhancements like arrow functions, classes, and modules, making JavaScript more expressive and maintainable.

Another pivotal moment in JavaScript's evolution was the rise of AJAX (Asynchronous JavaScript and XML) in the mid-2000s. AJAX allowed web pages to fetch data from servers without requiring a full page reload. This breakthrough technology revolutionized user experiences on the web, enabling dynamic content updates and interactive web applications. AJAX was a game-changer and laid the foundation for the single-page application (SPA) architecture, which has become increasingly popular in recent years.

As JavaScript's capabilities expanded, so did its ecosystem. A multitude of libraries and frameworks emerged to simplify and streamline web development. jQuery, for example, became immensely popular for its ability to simplify DOM manipulation and AJAX requests, making it easier for developers to create interactive web pages. In the realm of front-end frameworks, Angular, React, and Vue.js have gained prominence, each offering unique approaches to building web applications.

On the server side, Node.js emerged as a game-changing technology, allowing developers to use JavaScript for server-side programming. Node.js leverages the V8 JavaScript engine (developed by Google) and provides a non-blocking, event-driven architecture that is well-suited for handling concurrent connections and building scalable web applications. This convergence of client-side and server-side JavaScript has fostered the concept of full-stack development, enabling developers to work on both ends of a web application using a single language.

JavaScript's influence has also extended beyond the web, with frameworks like React Native and Electron enabling developers to build cross-platform mobile apps and desktop applications using the same JavaScript skills. This versatility has made JavaScript one of the most sought-after programming languages in the world, with a vast and active developer community.

In addition to its versatility, JavaScript has seen continuous performance improvements. Modern JavaScript engines, like V8 (used in Google Chrome) and SpiderMonkey (used in Firefox), employ sophisticated optimization techniques, such as Just-In-Time (JIT) compilation, to execute JavaScript code blazingly fast. This has enabled web applications to handle complex tasks and deliver responsive user experiences.

While JavaScript's journey has been largely positive, it hasn't been without its challenges. The language has faced criticism for certain quirks and inconsistencies, often referred to as "JavaScript's bad parts." However, efforts to improve the language have led to the development of tools like ESLint and TypeScript, which help developers catch errors and enforce coding standards. TypeScript, in particular, adds static typing to JavaScript, enhancing code quality and maintainability.

In recent years, JavaScript has become a foundational skill for web developers. Learning resources, such as online courses, tutorials, and documentation, have proliferated, making it more accessible to newcomers. JavaScript's open and inclusive community has also contributed to its growth, with conferences, meetups, and online forums providing platforms for knowledge sharing and collaboration.

Looking ahead, JavaScript's future appears promising. The ECMAScript specification continues to evolve, with new features and improvements regularly being introduced. Progressive Web Apps (PWAs) are gaining traction, offering offline capabilities and a native app-like experience using web technologies, further expanding JavaScript's domain. Additionally, the rise of WebAssembly (Wasm) promises to bring even more performance and versatility to web applications by allowing code written in languages like C++ and Rust to run in the browser alongside JavaScript.

In summary, JavaScript's journey from its humble beginnings to its current prominence in web development is a testament to its adaptability and enduring relevance. As the web continues to evolve, JavaScript will remain a crucial tool in the arsenal of developers, enabling them to create innovative and interactive experiences for users across the globe. With ongoing advancements and a vibrant community, JavaScript's role in shaping the future of the web is bound to continue expanding, making it an exciting and essential language for developers worldwide.

JavaScript matters in web development because it is the key programming language for creating dynamic and interactive web applications. It allows developers to add functionality to websites that can respond to user actions in real-time, providing a rich and engaging user experience. The importance of JavaScript in web development cannot be overstated, as it empowers developers to build everything from simple form validation to complex single-page applications (SPAs) and online games.

JavaScript is a client-side scripting language, meaning it runs in the user's web browser rather than on a remote server. This client-side execution enables JavaScript to work seamlessly with HTML and CSS, the other fundamental technologies of web development. Together, these three technologies form the foundation of the modern web, enabling developers to create dynamic and interactive websites and web applications that were once only possible through native desktop applications.

One of the key reasons why JavaScript matters in web development is its versatility. It is not limited to a specific type of web application but can be used in a wide range of contexts. Whether you're building a blog, an e-commerce platform, a social media site, or a real-time collaborative tool, JavaScript can be applied effectively. This adaptability has made JavaScript an essential tool for web developers, as it can handle a wide variety of tasks and solve different types of problems.

JavaScript's role in enhancing user interactivity is another reason why it matters in web development. Through JavaScript, developers can create features like interactive forms that validate user input, image sliders that respond to touch or mouse gestures, and dynamic content loading without requiring a full page refresh. These capabilities greatly improve the user experience and contribute to the success of modern web applications.

Furthermore, JavaScript plays a vital role in handling asynchronous operations, such as fetching data from servers, making API calls, and handling user interactions without blocking the user interface. This is achieved through mechanisms like AJAX (Asynchronous JavaScript and XML) and the Fetch API. As a result, JavaScript enables web applications to load and update data dynamically, providing users with real-time information and reducing the need for constant page reloads.

In the realm of modern web development, JavaScript frameworks and libraries have become indispensable tools. Frameworks like React, Angular, and Vue.js offer developers pre-built components, state management solutions, and routing systems that streamline the development process. These frameworks enable developers to build SPAs and maintain complex user interfaces with ease, making them essential for building feature-rich web applications efficiently.

Moreover, JavaScript's community-driven ecosystem is a testament to its importance in web development. An extensive ecosystem of open-source libraries and packages is available through package managers like npm and Yarn. These libraries cover a wide range of functionalities, from data manipulation and charting to authentication and user interface design. This ecosystem accelerates development by allowing developers to leverage existing solutions and focus on the unique aspects of their projects.

JavaScript's role extends beyond the client-side. With the advent of server-side JavaScript using technologies like Node.js, developers can use JavaScript for both the front-end and back-end development of web applications. This full-stack capability simplifies the development process and encourages code reuse, making it easier to maintain and scale web applications.

Another reason why JavaScript matters in web development is its continuous evolution. The language is constantly improving, with new features and enhancements being added through the ECMAScript specification. Each new version brings improved syntax, performance optimizations, and additional capabilities that empower developers to create more efficient and feature-rich web applications.

The importance of JavaScript in web development also extends to the field of mobile app development. Frameworks like React Native and technologies like Progressive Web Apps (PWAs) enable developers to use JavaScript to build cross-platform mobile applications. This approach allows for code sharing between web and mobile applications, reducing development time and effort while reaching a broader audience.

In the context of web development, JavaScript's ability to handle user input and manipulate the Document Object Model (DOM) is crucial. The DOM represents the structured representation of a web page, and JavaScript provides the means to interact with and modify it dynamically. This capability allows developers to create responsive web applications that adapt to user actions, providing a seamless and enjoyable user experience.

Security is another aspect of web development where JavaScript plays a vital role. With the ability to execute code in the user's browser, JavaScript must be used responsibly to prevent security vulnerabilities like Cross-Site Scripting (XSS) attacks. Developers must adhere to best practices, such as input validation, escaping output, and using secure authentication methods, to ensure the security of their web applications.

Furthermore, JavaScript's popularity and demand in the job market make it an essential skill for web developers. Employers actively seek developers proficient in JavaScript, and many job opportunities in web development require expertise in the language. Learning JavaScript not only opens doors to a wide range of career opportunities but also provides a solid foundation for mastering other programming languages and technologies.

In summary, JavaScript matters in web development because it is the linchpin that enables dynamic and interactive web experiences. Its versatility, interactivity, and continuous evolution make it an indispensable tool for building modern web applications. Whether you're a seasoned developer or just starting your journey in web development, JavaScript is a fundamental language that empowers you to create engaging and innovative web experiences for users worldwide. Its significance in the web development landscape is undeniable, and its relevance is poised to continue growing as the web evolves.

Chapter 2: Setting Up Your Development Environment

Choosing a text editor or Integrated Development Environment (IDE) is a crucial decision for any developer embarking on their coding journey. Your choice of coding environment can greatly impact your productivity, code quality, and overall development experience. To make an informed decision, it's essential to understand the differences between text editors and IDEs and consider your specific needs and preferences.

A text editor is a lightweight software tool designed primarily for editing plain text files. It provides essential features such as syntax highlighting, code autocompletion, and basic file management capabilities. Text editors are often minimalistic and highly customizable, allowing you to tailor the environment to your liking. They are a popular choice among developers who value simplicity and prefer to assemble their development toolkit by adding plugins or extensions as needed.

On the other hand, an Integrated Development Environment (IDE) is a comprehensive software package that includes a text editor, a debugger, a build automation tool, and other features, all integrated into a single application. IDEs are designed to offer a seamless development experience by providing a unified environment for coding, testing, debugging, and deploying applications. They often come with built-in support for specific programming languages or frameworks, making them a powerful choice for developers who work extensively with particular technologies.

When choosing between a text editor and an IDE, it's essential to consider your programming needs and workflow. If you're working on a small project, frequently switch between different languages, or prefer a minimalistic approach, a text editor may be a suitable choice. Text editors like Visual Studio Code, Sublime Text, and Atom have gained popularity for their flexibility and extensive plugin ecosystems, allowing developers to customize their environments to meet specific requirements.

However, if you're working on a large-scale project or using a language or framework that benefits from a robust development environment, an IDE may be the better option. IDEs like Visual Studio, IntelliJ IDEA, and PyCharm are well-suited for projects that demand features like code refactoring, integrated debugging, and seamless integration with version control systems. They often provide templates, code generators, and project management tools to streamline development tasks.

The choice between a text editor and an IDE also depends on your familiarity with the development ecosystem and your personal preferences. Developers who are comfortable with command-line tools and prefer to have fine-grained control over their development setup may lean towards text editors. In contrast, those who appreciate a more structured and integrated development experience may gravitate towards IDEs.

Another critical consideration when selecting a coding environment is the programming language you primarily work with. Some languages have dedicated IDEs that offer extensive language-specific features and optimizations. For example, if you're a Java developer, tools like Eclipse and NetBeans are tailored to the Java ecosystem and provide robust support for Java development. Similarly, languages like Python have specialized IDEs like PyCharm that offer advanced Python-centric features.

Accessibility and community support are also essential factors to evaluate. The availability of documentation, tutorials, and a vibrant user community can significantly impact your ability to learn and master your chosen environment. Popular text editors and IDEs often have large user bases and extensive online resources, making it easier to find help, plugins, and extensions to enhance your workflow.

Another aspect to consider is cross-platform compatibility. If you work on multiple operating systems or collaborate with developers who use different platforms, you may want to choose a coding environment that is available and performs consistently across various operating systems. Many popular text editors and IDEs offer versions for Windows, macOS, and Linux, ensuring compatibility and flexibility.

The extensibility and plugin ecosystem of your chosen coding environment can greatly enhance your productivity. Text editors like Visual Studio Code and

Sublime Text have vast libraries of community-contributed plugins that extend their functionality. These plugins can add support for specific languages, provide version control integration, enhance code formatting, and offer advanced debugging capabilities. IDEs also offer plugins but often focus on providing comprehensive features and integrations specific to their target languages and frameworks.

Performance is another critical factor to consider. While text editors are generally lightweight and responsive, some IDEs can be resource-intensive, particularly when handling large projects. It's essential to assess whether your development machine can handle the demands of the chosen coding environment without significant performance issues.

Collaboration and team workflow requirements should also influence your decision. If you work on projects with multiple team members, version control integration is crucial. Many coding environments, whether text editors or IDEs, support popular version control systems like Git, making it easier to collaborate on code with teammates. Additionally, the ability to configure coding style and linting rules can help maintain code consistency within your team.

Ultimately, your choice of a coding environment should align with your development goals and preferences. Some developers prefer the flexibility and simplicity of text editors, while others value the comprehensive features and integration offered by IDEs. It's essential to experiment with different tools, gather feedback from peers, and explore the available resources to make an informed decision.

In practice, many developers use a combination of tools. They might use a text editor for quick edits or lightweight tasks and switch to an IDE for more substantial projects or when working with specific languages or frameworks. This hybrid approach allows developers to leverage the strengths of both coding environments while adapting to the unique requirements of each project.

In summary, the choice between a text editor and an Integrated Development Environment (IDE) is a significant decision for any developer. It depends on various factors, including your programming needs, familiarity with the ecosystem, and personal preferences. Text editors offer flexibility and customization, making them suitable for diverse workflows, while IDEs provide comprehensive features and integrated development environments tailored to specific languages or frameworks. Ultimately, the best coding environment is one that aligns with your development goals and enhances your productivity and coding experience.

Installing and configuring Node.js and npm is a fundamental step for any developer looking to work with JavaScript on the server side or manage JavaScript packages for their projects. Node.js is a runtime environment that allows you to execute JavaScript code outside of a web browser, making it possible to build server-side applications, command-line tools, and more.

To begin the installation process, you'll need to download the appropriate Node.js installer for your operating system from the official Node.js website. Node.js offers installers for various platforms, including Windows, macOS, and Linux, making it accessible to developers regardless of their preferred operating system. Once you've downloaded the installer, follow the installation instructions specific to your operating system to complete the installation. Node.js also includes npm, which stands for "Node Package Manager," as a package manager for managing JavaScript libraries and dependencies. After the installation is complete, you can open your terminal or command prompt and run the following commands to verify that Node.js and npm are properly installed:

Copy code

```
node -v npm -v
```

These commands will display the installed Node.js and npm versions, respectively, confirming that the installation was successful. Node.js and npm are frequently updated to include bug fixes, new features, and security patches, so it's important to keep them up to date. To update Node.js and npm to the latest versions, you can use npm itself by running the following commands:

Copy code

```
npm install -g n n latest
```

The first command installs a package called "n," which is a version manager for Node.js. The second command uses "n" to switch to the latest available version of Node.js. This process ensures that you have the most

up-to-date Node.js runtime. You can also update npm to the latest version by running the following command:
cssCopy code

npm install -g npm @latest

This command installs the latest version of npm globally on your system. Managing multiple versions of Node.js on your machine can be essential for compatibility with different projects. Tools like "nvm" (Node Version Manager) for Linux/macOS or "nvm-windows" for Windows allow you to switch between Node.js versions easily. To install "nvm," you can follow the installation instructions provided in the official documentation for your specific operating system. Once "nvm" is installed, you can use it to install and manage multiple Node.js versions on your machine. For example, you can install a specific Node.js version using the following command:
phpCopy code

nvm install <node_version>

Replace "<node_version>" with the desired version number, such as "14.17.0." You can then switch between installed Node.js versions with the following command:
perlCopy code

nvm use <node_version>

This command sets the selected Node.js version as the active one for your current terminal session. To make a specific Node.js version the default for new terminal sessions, you can use the following command:
csharpCopy code

nvm alias default <node_version>

Node.js also comes with a built-in package manager called npm, which is used to install and manage JavaScript packages and dependencies for your projects. npm is incredibly versatile, allowing you to install packages globally or locally, manage project dependencies, and execute scripts defined in a project's package.json file. One of the first things you'll want to do after installing Node.js and npm is to configure npm with your own settings. You can do this by running the following command and following the prompts:
csharpCopy code

```
npm init
```

This command initializes a new npm project and creates a package.json file where you can specify project details, dependencies, and scripts. The prompts will ask you for information such as the project name, version, description, entry point, test command, and more. You can choose to accept the default values or customize them according to your project's needs. Once the package.json file is created, you can edit it directly to add or modify project information. For instance, you can add dependencies by running npm commands like:
goCopy code

```
npm install package-name
```

This command installs the specified package and adds it to the "dependencies" section of your package.json file. To add development-only dependencies, you can use the "--save-dev" flag, like this:
luaCopy code

```
npm install package-name --save-dev
```

This places the package in the "devDependencies" section of your package.json file, indicating that it's required for development purposes only. Managing dependencies with npm also includes updating packages to newer versions when necessary. You can use the following command to update a package to the latest version:

goCopy code

```
npm update package-name
```

This command updates the specified package to the latest available version and updates the version number in your package.json file. For more precise control over package versions, you can specify version ranges in your package.json file. For example, you can use the "^" symbol followed by a major version number to allow updates to minor and patch versions, like this:

jsonCopy code

```
"dependencies": { "package-name": "^1.0.0" }
```

This means that npm will install the latest version within the "1.x.x" range when you run "npm install." Another important aspect of configuring npm is setting up your npm registry. The default registry is the public npm registry, which contains a vast collection of open-source JavaScript packages. However, some organizations may have their private npm registries to host proprietary or custom packages. You can configure npm to use a different registry by running the following command:

arduinoCopy code

```
npm config set registry <registry_url>
```

Replace "<registry_url>" with the URL of your preferred npm registry. This command sets the registry for the current user, and npm will use this registry for all package installations and updates. If your organization requires authentication to access a private registry, you can use the following command to log in and save your authentication token:

Copy code

```
npm login
```

This command prompts you for your username, password, and email address associated with the registry. Once you've logged in, npm stores your authentication token securely, allowing you to install packages from the private registry without having to log in each time. In addition to configuring npm globally, you can also configure individual project settings using a .npmrc file. This file allows you to specify per-project configuration, such as the registry, proxy settings, and other npm options. By creating a .npmrc file in your project's root directory and adding configuration settings, you can ensure that your project uses the appropriate settings when others work on it. For example, you can create a .npmrc file with the following content:

arduinoCopy code

```
registry=https://your-private-registry-url/
```

This configuration will override the global registry settings for the specific project, ensuring that npm installs packages from the specified private registry. In summary, installing and configuring Node.js and npm is a fundamental step for JavaScript developers. Node.js provides the runtime environment for executing JavaScript on the server side, while npm serves as a powerful package manager for managing JavaScript dependencies. The installation process is straightforward, and it's essential to keep Node.js and npm up to date to benefit from the latest features, bug fixes, and security updates. Managing multiple Node.js versions using tools like "nvm" can help you work on various projects with different requirements. Configuring npm is equally important, allowing you to customize settings, manage project dependencies, and set up authentication for private registries. Whether you're building web applications, server-side APIs, or command-line tools, having Node.js and npm properly installed and configured is a crucial foundation for your JavaScript development journey.

Declaring variables is a fundamental concept in programming, allowing you to store and manipulate data in your code. In JavaScript, there are three ways to declare variables: using the "var," "let," and "const" keywords. The "var" keyword was traditionally used in JavaScript to declare variables, and it has some unique behavior compared to "let" and "const." When you declare a variable with "var," it is function-scoped, meaning it is only accessible within the function where it's declared or at the global scope if declared outside of any function. One notable feature of "var" is that it allows variable hoisting, which means that the variable declaration is moved to the top of its containing function or global scope during compilation, regardless of where it appears in the code. This behavior can lead to unexpected results if you're not careful, as variables declared with "var" can be used before their actual declaration in the code. For example, consider the following code snippet:

javascriptCopy code

```
console.log(myVar);  // Outputs "undefined"  var myVar = 42;
```

In this case, "myVar" is hoisted to the top of its containing scope, so the "console.log" statement doesn't result in an error, but the variable is initially "undefined." The "let" keyword was introduced in ECMAScript 2015 (ES6) and provides block-scoping, which means that variables declared with "let" are only accessible within the block or statement where they are defined. Block-scoped variables with "let" do not exhibit hoisting behavior, making it easier to understand variable scope and behavior. Here's an example using "let":

javascriptCopy code

```
{ let myVar = 42; console.log(myVar); // Outputs 42 }
console.log(myVar); // Throws an error: "myVar is not defined"
```

In this example, "myVar" is limited in scope to the block where it is declared, and attempting to access it outside of that block results in an error. The "const" keyword, also introduced in ES6, is used to declare variables whose values should not be reassigned after their initial assignment. Variables declared with "const" are block-scoped like "let," and they also do not exhibit hoisting behavior. A "const" variable must be initialized when declared, and once assigned a value, it cannot be changed or reassigned. Here's an example using "const":

luaCopy code

```
const pi = 3.14159265359; console.log(pi); // Outputs 3.14159265359 pi = 42; // Throws an error: "Assignment to constant variable"
```

In this case, "pi" is declared as a constant with an initial value, and any attempt to reassign it later in the code will result in an error. It's important to note that while "const" prevents the variable from being reassigned, it does not make objects or arrays declared with "const" immutable. For example:

scssCopy code

```
const myArray = [1, 2, 3]; myArray.push(4); // This is allowed myArray[0] = 0; // This is allowed
```

In this example, "myArray" is declared as a constant, but you can still modify its contents by adding elements or changing existing values within the array. To create an immutable object or array, you would need to use additional techniques like Object.freeze() or immutable data structures. When choosing between "var," "let," and "const," it's essential to consider the scope and mutability requirements of your variables. If a variable needs to be accessible within a specific block of code, consider using "let" or "const" for block-scoped behavior. If a variable should not be reassigned after its initial value is set, use "const" to convey your intent and prevent accidental reassignment. Avoid using "var" in modern JavaScript code, as it can lead to unexpected behavior due to hoisting and lack of block-scoping. Furthermore, it's good practice to use meaningful variable names that convey the purpose of the variable in your code, making it more readable and maintainable. For example, instead of naming a variable "x," use a descriptive name like "counter" or "total" to enhance the clarity of your code. Additionally, you can use camelCase or snake_case naming conventions for variables to improve code consistency and readability. JavaScript's flexibility in variable declaration allows you to choose the appropriate keyword ("var," "let," or "const") based on your specific programming needs and the scope of your variables. By understanding the differences and behaviors associated with each keyword, you can write more predictable and maintainable JavaScript code.

Working with data types is a fundamental aspect of programming, and JavaScript provides developers with a range of primitive and reference data types to handle different kinds of data. Primitive data types are the simplest data types in JavaScript and include numbers, strings, booleans, null, and undefined. Numbers in JavaScript can represent both integers and floating-point numbers, allowing you to perform various mathematical operations and calculations with ease. Strings are sequences of characters enclosed in single (''), double ("") or backticks (`) quotes, and they are used for representing textual data. Booleans, on the other hand, can only have two values: true or false, making them suitable for logical operations and conditional statements. The null data type represents the intentional absence of any object or value, while undefined indicates that a variable has been declared but has not been assigned a value. Primitive data types are immutable, meaning their values cannot be changed once they are assigned. Variables that hold primitive data types store the actual value in memory, allowing for simple and predictable behavior. For example, if you assign the number 42 to a variable, that variable will always hold the value 42 until it is reassigned. Reference data types, on the other hand, are more complex data types and include objects, arrays, functions, and more.

Objects in JavaScript are collections of key-value pairs, where keys are strings (or Symbols) and values can be of any data type, including other objects. Arrays are a special type of object that store an ordered list of values, which can be of different data types, and are accessed by their index. Functions are also reference data types, and they allow you to define reusable blocks of code that can be executed when invoked. Reference data types differ from primitive types in how they are stored and passed between variables and functions. Variables that hold reference data types do not store the actual data but rather a reference (or memory address) to where the data is stored in memory. This distinction has important implications for working with reference data types in JavaScript. When you assign a reference data type to a new variable or pass it as an argument to a function, you are working with a reference to the same underlying data. This means that if you modify the data through one variable, it will affect all other variables referencing the same data. For example, if you have two variables referencing the same array and you push a new value into the array using one variable, the change will be visible when accessing the array through the other variable as well. Understanding the difference between primitive and reference data types is crucial when working with JavaScript, as it can help you avoid unexpected behavior in your code. In JavaScript, variables declared with "var," "let," or "const" can hold both primitive and reference data types. When you declare a variable without assigning a value, JavaScript sets its initial value to "undefined." For example, if you declare a variable with "let" but don't assign a value, it will be initialized as "undefined."

javascriptCopy code

```
let myVar; console.log(myVar); // Outputs "undefined"
```

You can explicitly assign "null" to a variable if you want to indicate that it intentionally has no value. Primitive data types are assigned by value, which means that when you assign a primitive value to a variable or pass it as an argument to a function, a copy of the value is made, and any changes made to the variable or function parameter do not affect the original value. For example:

cssCopy code

```
let a = 42; let b = a; // 'b' now holds a copy of the value 42 b = 24; // Changing 'b' does not affect 'a' console.log(a); // Outputs 42
```

In this case, changing the value of "b" does not impact the value of "a" because primitive data types are assigned by value. Reference data types, on the other hand, are assigned by reference. When you assign a reference data type to a variable or pass it as an argument to a function, you are working with a reference to the underlying data. This means that changes made to the data through one variable will affect all other variables referencing the same data. For example:

sqlCopy code

```
let arr1 = [1, 2, 3]; let arr2 = arr1; // 'arr2' now references the same array as 'arr1' arr2.push(4); //
```

Modifying 'arr2' also modifies 'arr1' console.log(arr1); // Outputs [1, 2, 3, 4]

In this case, both "arr1" and "arr2" reference the same array, so changes made to one affect the other. When working with reference data types, it's essential to be mindful of this behavior to avoid unintended side effects in your code. You can create a true copy (or clone) of an array or object to avoid modifying the original data by using various methods, such as the spread operator or the Object.assign() method for objects.

scssCopy code

```
// Creating a copy of an array using the spread operator
let originalArray = [1, 2, 3]; let copiedArray = [...originalArray]; copiedArray.push(4); // Modifying 'copiedArray' does not affect 'originalArray' console.log(originalArray); // Outputs [1, 2, 3]
```

javascriptCopy code

```
// Creating a copy of an object using Object.assign() let originalObject = { name: "John", age: 30 }; let copiedObject = Object.assign({}, originalObject); copiedObject.age = 40; // Modifying 'copiedObject' does not affect 'originalObject' console.log(originalObject); // Outputs { name: 'John', age: 30 }
```

In addition to objects and arrays, functions in JavaScript are also reference data types. When you pass a function as an argument to another function, you are passing a reference to the original function, allowing you to invoke it from within the receiving function. This behavior enables powerful patterns like callback functions and event handling in JavaScript.

scssCopy code

```
function greet(name) { console.log(`Hello, ${name}!`); } function sayHello(callback) { callback("John"); } sayHello(greet); // Outputs "Hello, John!"
```

In this example, the "sayHello" function takes a callback function as an argument and invokes it with the name "John." Understanding how primitive and reference data types work in JavaScript is essential for writing reliable and bug-free code. By recognizing the differences in how data is stored and passed between variables and functions, you can make informed decisions about when to use primitive types and when to work with reference types. This knowledge is foundational for mastering JavaScript and building robust applications that manipulate and manage data effectively.

Chapter 4: Control Flow: Conditional Statements and Loops

Using if...else statements is a fundamental aspect of programming that allows you to control the flow of your code based on conditions. Conditional statements are essential for making decisions in your programs, and JavaScript provides several ways to implement them. The most basic form of a conditional statement is the if statement, which allows you to execute a block of code if a specified condition evaluates to true. For example, you can use an if statement to check if a user's age is greater than or equal to 18 and display a message accordingly.

javascriptCopy code

```javascript
let age = 20; if (age >= 18) { console.log("You are an adult."); }
```

In this example, the condition "age >= 18" is evaluated, and since it is true, the code inside the curly braces is executed, resulting in the message "You are an adult" being displayed. You can also use the else statement to provide an alternative block of code to execute when the condition in the if statement evaluates to false. For instance, you can modify the previous example to include an else statement to handle the case when the user is not an adult.

javascriptCopy code

```
let age = 15; if (age >= 18) { console.log("You are an
adult."); } else { console.log("You are not an adult.");
}
```

Now, when the user's age is less than 18, the code
inside the else block is executed, and the message "You
are not an adult" is displayed. In addition to if and else,
you can use else if statements to evaluate multiple
conditions sequentially. This allows you to check
different conditions and execute the corresponding
code block for the first condition that evaluates to true.
Here's an example that uses else if to check whether a
number is positive, negative, or zero:

typescriptCopy code

```
let number = 5; if (number > 0) { console.log("The
number is positive."); } else if (number < 0) {
console.log("The number is negative."); } else {
console.log("The number is zero."); }
```

In this case, the code inside the first if block is executed
because the number is greater than zero. If the number
were negative, the code inside the else if block would
run, and if the number were zero, the code inside the
else block would execute. Conditional statements can
also be nested within each other to create more
complex decision-making logic. For example, you can
use nested if statements to check multiple conditions,
as demonstrated in the following code snippet:

javascriptCopy code

```
let x = 10; let y = 5; if (x > 0) { if (y > 0) {
console.log("Both x and y are positive."); } else {
```

console.log("x is positive, but y is not."); } } else { console.log("x is not positive."); }

In this example, the outer if statement checks if x is positive, and if it is, the inner if statement checks if y is positive. Depending on the values of x and y, different messages are displayed. While if...else statements provide a way to make decisions based on conditions, JavaScript also offers a ternary operator as a concise alternative for simple conditional expressions. The ternary operator, also known as the conditional operator, allows you to write a conditional expression in a single line of code. Here's an example that uses the ternary operator to determine if a person is eligible to vote based on their age:

javascriptCopy code

```
let age = 20; let isEligibleToVote = age >= 18 ? "Yes" : "No"; console.log(`Is eligible to vote? ${isEligibleToVote}`);
```

In this example, the condition "age >= 18" is evaluated, and if it's true, the value "Yes" is assigned to the variable isEligibleToVote; otherwise, "No" is assigned. Using the ternary operator can make your code more concise and readable, especially for simple conditional assignments. However, it's essential to use it judiciously and consider readability when dealing with more complex conditions. When working with conditional statements, you may encounter scenarios where you want to execute specific code when multiple conditions are met simultaneously. In such cases, you can use logical operators such as && (logical AND) and ||

(logical OR) to combine conditions. The && operator requires both conditions to be true for the overall condition to evaluate as true. Here's an example that checks if a number is both positive and even:

typescriptCopy code

```
let number = 6; if (number > 0 && number % 2 === 0) { console.log("The number is positive and even."); }
```

In this example, both conditions "number > 0" and "number % 2 === 0" must be true for the code inside the if statement to execute. The || operator, on the other hand, requires at least one of the conditions to be true for the overall condition to evaluate as true. Here's an example that checks if a person is eligible to vote based on age or citizenship:

javascriptCopy code

```
let age = 17; let isCitizen = false; if (age >= 18 || isCitizen) { console.log("The person is eligible to vote."); }
```

In this case, if either "age >= 18" or "isCitizen" is true, the code inside the if statement will run. You can also use the logical NOT operator (!) to negate a condition. For example, to check if a number is not equal to zero, you can write:

typescriptCopy code

```
let number = 5; if (!(number === 0)) { console.log("The number is not zero."); }
```

In this example, the condition inside the if statement is negated using the ! operator, so the code block executes when the number is not equal to zero. Conditional statements are a powerful tool in programming, allowing you to create dynamic and responsive code that can adapt to different situations. By mastering if...else statements and understanding how to combine conditions using logical operators, you can build more sophisticated and interactive JavaScript applications. Effective use of conditional statements enhances your ability to control the flow of your programs and make them behave precisely as intended based on various conditions and inputs.

Iterating, or looping, is a fundamental concept in programming that allows you to execute a block of code multiple times. Loops are essential for automating repetitive tasks, processing data collections, and handling various program flow scenarios. In JavaScript, two of the most commonly used types of loops are the "for" loop and the "while" loop, each serving its unique purpose. The "for" loop is particularly versatile and is often used when you know the number of iterations required in advance. Its basic structure consists of three parts: initialization, condition, and increment. Here's a typical example of a "for" loop that counts from 1 to 5: cssCopy code

```
for (let i = 1; i <= 5; i++) { console.log(i); }
```

In this example, the "for" loop initializes a variable "i" to 1, sets a condition "i <= 5" for the loop to continue running, and increments "i" by 1 after each iteration. The loop iterates five times, and with each iteration, it prints the value of "i" to the console. The output of this loop will be the numbers 1 through 5. The "while" loop, on the other hand, is more flexible and is often used when you don't know the exact number of iterations in advance. A "while" loop continues executing as long as a specified condition remains true. Here's an example of a "while" loop that counts from 1 to 5:

cssCopy code

```
let i = 1; while (i <= 5) { console.log(i); i++; }
```

In this "while" loop, we start by initializing the variable "i" to 1, and the loop continues as long as the condition "i <= 5" holds true. Inside the loop, we print the value of "i" to the console and increment it by 1. Just like the "for" loop, this "while" loop will also output the numbers 1 through 5. While both "for" and "while" loops can achieve similar results, choosing the right one depends on the specific requirements of your code and the problem you're solving. The "for" loop is often preferred when you have a predetermined number of iterations or need to iterate over a range of values, as it provides a concise and structured way to express such loops. The "while" loop, on the other hand, is suitable when you need to loop based on a condition that may change during execution, such as user input or data processing. To illustrate further, let's consider an example of using a "for" loop to iterate over an array of names and print each name to the console:

cssCopy code

```
const names = ["Alice", "Bob", "Charlie", "David", "Eve"]; for (let i = 0; i < names.length; i++) { console.log(names[i]); }
```

In this "for" loop, we initialize "i" to 0, set the condition as "i < names.length" (which is the length of the array), and increment "i" by 1 in each iteration. The loop prints each name in the "names" array to the console. Alternatively, let's use a "while" loop to accomplish the same task:

cssCopy code

```
const names = ["Alice", "Bob", "Charlie", "David", "Eve"]; let i = 0; while (i < names.length) { console.log(names[i]); i++; }
```

Here, we initialize "i" to 0 outside the loop, and the "while" loop continues as long as "i" is less than the length of the "names" array. Inside the loop, we print each name and increment "i" to move to the next element in the array. Both "for" and "while" loops can effectively iterate over arrays, but the choice between them often depends on your coding style and the specific use case. Another essential aspect of loops is the ability to control the flow of execution within a loop using control statements like "break" and "continue." The "break" statement allows you to exit a loop prematurely, even if the loop condition is still true. Consider this example, where a "for" loop iterates from 1 to 10 but breaks when it reaches the number 5:

cssCopy code

```
for (let i = 1; i <= 10; i++) { if (i === 5) { break; } console.log(i); }
```

In this case, the "break" statement is triggered when "i" equals 5, causing the loop to terminate immediately. As a result, only the numbers 1 through 4 are printed to the console. The "continue" statement, on the other hand, allows you to skip the current iteration of a loop and continue with the next iteration. Here's an example using "continue" to skip even numbers when printing the numbers from 1 to 10:

cssCopy code

```
for (let i = 1; i <= 10; i++) { if (i % 2 === 0) {
continue; } console.log(i); }
```

In this "for" loop, when "i" is an even number (i.e., "i % 2 === 0" is true), the "continue" statement is executed, skipping the rest of the code inside the loop for that iteration. As a result, only the odd numbers (1, 3, 5, 7, 9) are printed to the console. Understanding how to use "break" and "continue" statements can help you fine-tune the behavior of your loops and handle specific conditions or exceptions gracefully. Additionally, JavaScript provides more advanced looping constructs, such as "for...of" and "for...in" loops, which are particularly useful when working with arrays and objects. The "for...of" loop is designed for iterating over the values of an iterable object, such as an array or a string. Here's an example of using a "for...of" loop to iterate over an array of colors:

arduinoCopy code

```
const colors = ["red", "green", "blue"]; for (const
color of colors) { console.log(color); }
```

In this "for...of" loop, the variable "color" takes on each value in the "colors" array during each iteration. The loop simplifies the process of iterating over elements without the need for an index variable like "i." The "for...in" loop, on the other hand, is used to iterate over the enumerable properties of an object. Here's an example of using a "for...in" loop to iterate over the properties of an object:

vbnetCopy code

```
const person = { name: "Alice", age: 30, gender: "female" }; for (const key in person) { console.log(key + ": " + person[key]); }
```

In this "for...in" loop, the variable "key" represents each property name in the "person" object, allowing you to access the corresponding values. Loops are indispensable tools in programming, enabling you to automate repetitive tasks, process data efficiently, and control program flow based on conditions. Whether you choose the classic "for" and "while" loops or opt for more specialized constructs like "for...of" and "for...in" loops, mastering looping techniques is essential for becoming a proficient JavaScript developer. By understanding the differences between loop types and using control statements like "break" and "continue" effectively, you can write more efficient and expressive code, making your programs more powerful and versatile.

Chapter 5: Functions and Scope

Functions are a fundamental concept in programming, serving as reusable blocks of code that can be executed when needed. They are essential for organizing and modularizing code, making it more maintainable and efficient. In JavaScript, a function is defined using the "function" keyword, followed by a name, a list of parameters enclosed in parentheses, and a block of code enclosed in curly braces. Here's a basic example of a JavaScript function that adds two numbers together and returns the result:

javascriptCopy code

```
function add(a, b) { return a + b; }
```

In this function, "add" is the name of the function, and it takes two parameters, "a" and "b." The code inside the function calculates the sum of "a" and "b" using the "+" operator and returns the result. To call or invoke a function, you use its name followed by a pair of parentheses containing the arguments you want to pass to the function. Here's how you can call the "add" function:

javascriptCopy code

```
let result = add(3, 5); console.log(result); // Outputs 8
```

In this example, we call the "add" function with the arguments 3 and 5, and it returns the sum, which is then stored in the variable "result" and printed to the console. Functions in JavaScript can also be defined without parameters, like this:

javascriptCopy code

```
function sayHello() { console.log("Hello, world!"); }
```

This "sayHello" function doesn't take any parameters and simply logs the message "Hello, world!" to the console when called. You can call it as follows:

javascriptCopy code

```
sayHello(); // Outputs "Hello, world!"
```

Functions can have optional parameters, which means you can call them with or without arguments. Inside the function, you can check if a parameter is defined or use default values if it's not provided. Here's an example of a function with optional parameters that calculates the area of a rectangle:

javascriptCopy code

```
function calculateArea(width, height) { if (width === undefined || height === undefined) { return "Please provide both width and height."; } return width * height; }
```

In this function, we first check if either "width" or "height" is undefined, and if so, we return a message asking the user to provide both values. Otherwise, we calculate the area by multiplying "width" and "height." You can call this function with both values or just one:

javascriptCopy code

```
console.log(calculateArea(3, 4)); // Outputs 12
console.log(calculateArea(5)); // Outputs "Please provide both width and height."
```

Functions can also return different types of values, not just numbers or strings. They can return other functions, objects, arrays, or even undefined if there is no explicit return statement. Here's an example of a function that returns another function:

javascriptCopy code

```
function createMultiplier(factor) { return function (number) { return number * factor; }; }
```

In this example, the "createMultiplier" function takes a "factor" as an argument and returns a new function. The returned function takes another argument, "number," and multiplies it by the "factor" provided when creating the multiplier function. You can use it to create custom multiplier functions:

javascriptCopy code

```
const double = createMultiplier(2); const triple = createMultiplier(3); console.log(double(5)); // Outputs 10 console.log(triple(5)); // Outputs 15
```

In this code, we create two multiplier functions, "double" and "triple," by calling "createMultiplier" with different factors. Then, we use these custom multiplier functions to multiply numbers by their respective factors. Functions in JavaScript can also be assigned to variables, making them first-class citizens in the language. This means you can treat functions like any other data type, passing them as arguments to other functions, returning them from functions, and storing them in variables. Here's an example of a function assigned to a variable:

javascriptCopy code

```
const greet = function (name) { console.log(`Hello, ${name}!`); };
```

In this example, we define an anonymous function and assign it to the variable "greet." You can call the "greet" function just like any other function:

javascriptCopy code

```
greet("Alice"); // Outputs "Hello, Alice!"
```

This pattern is commonly used for creating callback functions or passing functions as arguments to higher-order functions. JavaScript also supports arrow functions, which provide a concise syntax for defining functions, especially when the function body consists of a single expression. Here's an example of an arrow function that squares a number:

javascriptCopy code

```
const square = (x) => x * x;
```

In this arrow function, the parameter "x" is followed by the arrow "=>" and the expression "x * x." Arrow functions can be especially useful when working with arrays and higher-order functions like "map," "filter," and "reduce." For instance, here's how you can use an arrow function with "map" to square each number in an array:

javascriptCopy code

```
const numbers = [1, 2, 3, 4, 5]; const
squaredNumbers = numbers.map((x) => x * x);
console.log(squaredNumbers); // Outputs [1, 4, 9, 16,
25]
```

In this code, the arrow function is used within the "map" method to transform each element in the "numbers" array by squaring it. Functions in JavaScript can also have side effects, which means they can modify variables, interact with the environment, or perform other actions beyond returning a value. For example, a function might update a global variable or manipulate the DOM of a web page. Here's an example of a function that has a side effect by modifying a global variable:

javascriptCopy code

```
let counter = 0; function incrementCounter() {
counter++; }
```

In this function, "incrementCounter" increments the global variable "counter" by 1 each time it's called. Side effects can make functions more versatile, but they can also introduce complexity and make code harder to reason about. It's essential to document side effects clearly and use them judiciously to maintain code clarity and predictability. In addition to regular functions, JavaScript also supports the concept of function expressions and anonymous functions. A function expression is a function that is defined within an expression, rather than a declaration. Here's an example of a function expression:

javascriptCopy code

```
const greet = function (name) { console.log(`Hello,
${name}!`); };
```

In this example, "greet" is a variable that holds an anonymous function, creating a function expression. Function expressions are often used when you need to define a function on the fly or pass it as an argument to another function. Anonymous functions, as the name suggests, don't have a name and are defined inline.

They are commonly used for short, one-off functions that won't be reused elsewhere in the code. Here's an example of an anonymous function:

javascriptCopy code

```
const numbers = [1, 2, 3, 4, 5]; const squaredNumbers = numbers.map(function (x) { return x * x; }); console.log(squaredNumbers); // Outputs [1, 4, 9, 16, 25]
```

In this code, an anonymous function is used within the "map" method to square each element in the "numbers" array. While anonymous functions are concise, they can be less readable than named functions, especially for complex logic. Choosing between named functions, function expressions, arrow functions, and anonymous functions depends on the specific use case and coding style. Functions can also be hoisted in JavaScript, which means you can call a function before it's defined in the code. JavaScript's function hoisting behavior allows you to write code in a way that makes logical sense, even if the function declarations appear later in the script. However, it's a good practice to define your functions before calling them to improve code clarity and avoid unexpected behavior. In summary, functions are a core building block of JavaScript, enabling you to encapsulate reusable code, make your programs more modular, and execute specific tasks. You can define functions with parameters and return values, assign them to variables, use arrow functions for concise expressions, and even create higher-order functions. Understanding how to define, call, and work with functions is essential for writing clean, maintainable, and efficient JavaScript code. Functions are a versatile tool in your programming toolkit, and mastering them is a crucial step toward becoming a proficient JavaScript developer.

To write effective JavaScript code, it's essential to understand the concepts of function scope and closures. These concepts play a crucial role in how variables are accessed and maintained in memory during the execution of your code. Function scope refers to the visibility and accessibility of variables within a specific function. In JavaScript, variables declared inside a function are said to have local scope, meaning they are only accessible within that function. This concept is often referred to as lexical scope, which means that the scope of a variable is determined by its location within the source code. Variables declared outside of any function, known as global variables, have a global scope and can be accessed from anywhere in your code. Let's illustrate this with an example:

```
javascriptCopy code
function outerFunction() { // This variable is only accessible within outerFunction const localVar = "I am a local variable."; function innerFunction() { // This variable is only accessible within innerFunction const innerVar = "I am another local variable."; console.log(localVar); // Accessing localVar from the outer function console.log(innerVar); // Accessing innerVar from the inner function } innerFunction(); }
```

outerFunction(); console.log(localVar); // This will result in an error since localVar is not accessible here

In this example, "localVar" is declared in the "outerFunction" and can only be accessed within that function. Similarly, "innerVar" is declared in the "innerFunction" and is only accessible within that function. Attempting to access these variables outside of their respective functions will result in an error. Understanding function scope is essential for preventing unintended variable collisions and maintaining clean and modular code. It allows you to encapsulate variables and logic within functions, reducing the risk of naming conflicts and unexpected behavior. Closures are closely related to function scope and are a powerful JavaScript feature that enables functions to "remember" the variables from their containing scope even after that scope has exited. In other words, closures allow a function to maintain access to its surrounding function's variables even when the outer function has finished executing. Consider the following example:

javascriptCopy code

```
function createCounter() { let count = 0; return function () { return ++count; }; } const counter = createCounter(); console.log(counter()); // Outputs 1
console.log(counter()); // Outputs 2
```

In this code, the "createCounter" function defines a local variable called "count" and returns an anonymous function that increments and returns the "count" variable each time it's called. When we call "createCounter," it returns the inner anonymous function, which is assigned to the "counter" variable. Even though "createCounter" has completed its execution, the inner function still maintains access to the "count" variable due to the closure. As a result, each time we invoke "counter," it continues incrementing the "count" variable as if it were still within the scope of "createCounter." Closures are incredibly useful for creating private variables and functions, as they allow you to encapsulate data and behavior within a specific context without exposing it to the global scope. They are frequently used in JavaScript libraries and frameworks to implement encapsulation and maintain state across multiple function calls. It's important to note that closures can also lead to memory leaks if not managed correctly. Since closures maintain references to their containing scope's variables, these variables cannot be garbage collected until the closure itself is no longer reachable. If you have closures that hold references to large objects or data structures, it can lead to increased memory consumption. To mitigate this, it's advisable to be mindful of the scope and lifetime of closures, and when they are no longer needed, consider nullifying their references or removing event listeners if they are associated with DOM elements. In addition to creating closures explicitly, JavaScript also has built-in functions that utilize closures, such as callbacks and event handlers. Callbacks are functions passed as arguments to other functions and are executed later, often after an asynchronous

operation has completed. Here's an example of a callback function used with the "setTimeout" function:
javascriptCopy code

```javascript
function greet(name, callback) { setTimeout(function
() { console.log(`Hello, ${name}!`); callback(); },
1000); } function sayGoodbye() {
console.log("Goodbye!"); } greet("Alice",
sayGoodbye);
```

In this example, the "greet" function accepts a name and a callback function. It uses "setTimeout" to delay the greeting message for one second, and then it calls the callback function, which says goodbye. Callbacks are often used in scenarios where you want to perform an action after some asynchronous operation, like fetching data from a server or reading a file. The closure in this case is the anonymous function passed to "setTimeout," which maintains access to the "name" variable from the outer scope, even after "greet" has completed. Event handlers are another common use case for closures in JavaScript. When you attach an event handler to a DOM element, the handler function often has access to variables and elements from the surrounding context. For example, consider the following code that adds click event handlers to a list of buttons:
javascriptCopy code

```javascript
const buttons =
document.querySelectorAll("button"); for (let i = 0; i
< buttons.length; i++) {
buttons[i].addEventListener("click", function () {
console.log(`Button ${i + 1} clicked.`); }); }
```

In this code, we loop through a list of buttons and attach a click event listener to each one. Inside the event listener function, we log a message that includes the button's index. The closure here is the function within the event listener, which maintains access to the "i" variable from the outer scope, even after the loop has completed. However, closures in event handlers can lead to unexpected behavior if you're not careful. In this case, clicking any button will log "Button 4 clicked" because the value of "i" becomes 4 by the time the event listener executes. To fix this issue and ensure that each button logs its respective index, you can create a new function scope for each iteration using an immediately invoked function expression (IIFE) or the "let" keyword:

javascriptCopy code

```
const buttons = document.querySelectorAll("button"); for (let i = 0; i < buttons.length; i++) { (function (index) { buttons[index].addEventListener("click", function () { console.log(`Button ${index + 1} clicked.`); }); })(i); }
```

In this revised code, we wrap the event listener function in an IIFE that takes the current value of "i" as an argument. This ensures that each event listener has its own copy of the index, resulting in the expected behavior when clicking the buttons. In summary, understanding function scope and closures is crucial for writing effective and maintainable JavaScript code. Function scope defines the visibility of variables within a function, while closures allow functions to maintain access to their containing scope's variables, even after the outer function has completed. Closures are powerful and commonly used in JavaScript for encapsulation, callbacks, and event handling. However, they can also lead to memory leaks if not managed properly, so it's important to be mindful of their usage. By mastering these concepts, you'll be better equipped to write clean, efficient, and bug-free JavaScript code.

Chapter 6: Working with Arrays and Objects

Arrays are fundamental data structures in JavaScript that allow you to store and manipulate collections of data. They provide a way to organize and work with lists of values, making them a crucial part of web development. In JavaScript, an array is an ordered list of elements, which can be of any data type, including numbers, strings, objects, or even other arrays. To create an array, you can use square brackets and place the elements you want to include inside them, separated by commas. Here's an example of creating an array of numbers:

javascriptCopy code

```
const numbers = [1, 2, 3, 4, 5];
```

In this example, we've created an array called "numbers" containing five integer values. Arrays can also hold a mix of data types, as shown in this example:

javascriptCopy code

```
const mixedArray = [1, 'two', { key: 'value' }, true];
```

In "mixedArray," we have integers, strings, an object, and a boolean value all within the same array. Once you have an array, you can access its elements by their index, with the first element at index 0, the second at index 1, and so on. For example, to access the first element of "numbers," you can use:

javascriptCopy code

```
const firstNumber = numbers[0];
```

Now, "firstNumber" contains the value 1. Arrays also have a "length" property that tells you how many elements are in the array:

```javascript
javascriptCopy code
const arrayLength = numbers.length;
```
In this case, "arrayLength" would be assigned the value 5 because there are five elements in the "numbers" array. Adding elements to an array is straightforward; you can use the "push" method to add an element to the end of an array:

```javascript
javascriptCopy code
numbers.push(6);
```
After this operation, the "numbers" array will contain [1, 2, 3, 4, 5, 6]. To remove the last element from an array, you can use the "pop" method:

```javascript
javascriptCopy code
numbers.pop();
```
Now, "numbers" will be [1, 2, 3, 4, 5] again. Arrays in JavaScript are also mutable, meaning you can change their elements directly by assigning new values to specific indices:

```javascript
javascriptCopy code
numbers[0] = 7;
```
This would change the first element of "numbers" to 7. Arrays provide various methods for manipulating their elements and performing common operations. One such method is "splice," which allows you to add, remove, or replace elements at specific positions within the array. Here's an example of using "splice" to add elements to an array:

```javascript
javascriptCopy code
numbers.splice(2, 0, 8, 9);
```
In this case, we start at index 2, remove 0 elements, and add the values 8 and 9, resulting in the "numbers" array

becoming [1, 2, 8, 9, 3, 4, 5]. If you want to remove elements using "splice," you specify the starting index and the number of elements to remove:

javascriptCopy code

```javascript
numbers.splice(3, 2);
```

This will remove two elements starting from index 3, leading to "numbers" containing [1, 2, 8, 5]. Another commonly used method is "slice," which creates a new array containing elements from a specified range of the original array without modifying the original array itself:

javascriptCopy code

```javascript
const slicedArray = numbers.slice(1, 4);
```

In this example, "slicedArray" will contain [2, 8, 5], as it includes elements from index 1 to 3 (excluding the element at index 4). Arrays can be sorted using the "sort" method, which arranges elements in ascending order by default:

javascriptCopy code

```javascript
numbers.sort();
```

After this operation, "numbers" will be [1, 2, 5, 8]. To sort elements in descending order, you can provide a compare function as an argument to "sort":

javascriptCopy code

```javascript
numbers.sort((a, b) => b - a);
```

Now, "numbers" will be [8, 5, 2, 1]. Arrays also support iteration through various methods, such as "forEach," "map," "filter," and "reduce." The "forEach" method allows you to execute a function for each element in the array:

javascriptCopy code

```
numbers.forEach((element) => { console.log(element);
});
```
This code will log each element of "numbers" to the console. The "map" method creates a new array by applying a function to each element of the original array:

javascriptCopy code
```
const doubledNumbers = numbers.map((element) =>
element * 2);
```
Here, "doubledNumbers" will contain [16, 10, 4, 2]. The "filter" method creates a new array containing elements that satisfy a condition:

javascriptCopy code
```
const evenNumbers = numbers.filter((element) =>
element % 2 === 0);
```
"evenNumbers" will contain [8, 2]. The "reduce" method allows you to accumulate values from an array into a single result:

javascriptCopy code
```
const sum = numbers.reduce((accumulator,
currentValue) => accumulator + currentValue, 0);
```
In this case, "sum" will be assigned the value 16, as it computes the sum of all elements in "numbers." Arrays in JavaScript also offer methods like "find," "some," and "every" for specific searching and validation tasks. The "find" method returns the first element in the array that satisfies a provided testing function:

javascriptCopy code
```
const firstEven = numbers.find((element) => element %
2 === 0);
```

In this example, "firstEven" will contain 8. The "some" method checks if at least one element in the array meets a given condition:

javascriptCopy code

```
const hasOddNumber = numbers.some((element) => element % 2 !== 0);
```

Here, "hasOddNumber" will be "true" because the array contains odd numbers. The "every" method verifies if all elements in the array satisfy a particular condition:

javascriptCopy code

```
const allEven = numbers.every((element) => element % 2 === 0);
```

In this case, "allEven" will be "false" because the array contains at least one odd number. JavaScript also provides ways to combine and manipulate arrays using methods like "concat," "join," and "slice." The "concat" method joins two or more arrays and returns a new array:

javascriptCopy code

```
const moreNumbers = [10, 20]; const combinedArray = numbers.concat(moreNumbers);
```

"combinedArray" will contain [8, 5, 2, 1, 10, 20]. The "join" method creates a string by concatenating all elements in the array with a specified separator:

javascriptCopy code

```
const arrayAsString = numbers.join(', ');
```

"arrayAsString" will be the string "8, 5, 2, 1." Arrays in JavaScript can also be multidimensional, allowing you to create arrays of arrays to represent more complex data structures. For example, you can create a two-dimensional array to represent a matrix:

javascriptCopy code

const matrix = [[1, 2, 3], [4, 5, 6], [7, 8, 9]];
In this "matrix" array, each element is itself an array representing a row of numbers. You can access individual elements within a multidimensional array by using multiple sets of square brackets:

```javascript
const value = matrix[1][2]; // Accessing the number 6
```

"value" will be 6 because it corresponds to the element at row 1 and column 2 of the "matrix." In summary, arrays are essential data structures in JavaScript that allow you to store, access, and manipulate collections of data. They provide various methods and techniques for adding, removing, and transforming elements within the array. Additionally, arrays support iteration and searching operations, making them a versatile tool for working with lists of values in your JavaScript applications.

In JavaScript, objects are a fundamental data type that allows you to store and manipulate structured data. Objects are collections of key-value pairs, where each key is a string (or symbol) and each value can be of any data type, including numbers, strings, functions, other objects, or even arrays. To create an object, you can use curly braces and define its properties and values within them. For example, here's how you can create an object representing a person's information:

```javascript
const person = { firstName: "John", lastName: "Doe", age: 30, isEmployed: true, };
```

In this example, "person" is an object with four properties: "firstName," "lastName," "age," and "isEmployed," each with corresponding values. You can access the values of object properties using dot notation or bracket notation.

For instance, to access the "firstName" property of the "person" object using dot notation:

javascriptCopy code

```
const firstName = person.firstName; // firstName contains "John"
```

Alternatively, you can use bracket notation with a string containing the property name:

javascriptCopy code

```
const lastName = person["lastName"]; // lastName contains "Doe"
```

Both dot notation and bracket notation work for accessing object properties, but bracket notation is more flexible and allows you to access properties with dynamic or computed names. For example, you can access a property using a variable:

javascriptCopy code

```
const propertyName = "age"; const age = person[propertyName]; // age contains 30
```

You can also use bracket notation to access properties with spaces or special characters in their names:

javascriptCopy code

```
const book = { "title with spaces": "JavaScript Guide", "author-name": "John Doe", }; const title = book["title with spaces"]; // title contains "JavaScript Guide" const author = book["author-name"]; // author contains "John Doe"
```

Objects in JavaScript are mutable, meaning you can modify their properties after creation. To change the value of a property, simply assign a new value to it:

javascriptCopy code

person.age = 35; // Updating the age property
person.isEmployed = false; // Changing the isEmployed property

After these assignments, the "person" object will have an updated age of 35 and an "isEmployed" property set to false. You can also add new properties to an object by simply assigning a value to a new key:

javascriptCopy code

person.city = "New York"; // Adding a new city property

Now, the "person" object includes a "city" property with the value "New York." To remove a property from an object, you can use the "delete" operator:

javascriptCopy code

delete person.city; // Removing the city property

After this operation, the "city" property will no longer exist in the "person" object. Objects can also contain methods, which are functions assigned as values to object properties. These methods can perform actions or computations related to the object's data. Here's an example of an object with a method:

javascriptCopy code

const calculator = { add: function (a, b) { return a + b; }, subtract: function (a, b) { return a - b; }, };

In this "calculator" object, there are two methods: "add" and "subtract." You can invoke these methods using dot notation:

javascriptCopy code

const sum = calculator.add(5, 3); // sum contains 8
const difference = calculator.subtract(10, 4); // difference contains 6

Methods can also access and modify the object's properties using the "this" keyword, which refers to the object itself. Here's an example of a method that uses "this" to access an object property:

javascriptCopy code

```
const person = { firstName: "John", lastName: "Doe", getFullName: function () { return this.firstName + " " + this.lastName; }, }; const fullName = person.getFullName(); // fullName contains "John Doe"
```

In the "getFullName" method, "this" is used to access the "firstName" and "lastName" properties of the "person" object, allowing it to return the full name. JavaScript also supports shorthand method notation, which allows you to define methods more concisely:

javascriptCopy code

```
const calculator = { add(a, b) { return a + b; }, subtract(a, b) { return a - b; }, };
```

In this updated "calculator" object, the methods are defined using the shorthand notation, which is a cleaner and more modern way to declare methods. When working with objects, you may encounter the need to iterate over their properties. You can achieve this using various techniques, such as "for...in" loops or built-in methods like "Object.keys," "Object.values," and "Object.entries." The "for...in" loop allows you to iterate over the keys (property names) of an object:

javascriptCopy code

```
for (const key in person) { console.log(key); // Outputs "firstName," "lastName," and other properties console.log(person[key]); // Outputs the corresponding values }
```

The "Object.keys" method returns an array of the object's property names:

javascriptCopy code

```
const keys = Object.keys(person); // keys contains ["firstName", "lastName", ...]
```

You can then use this array to iterate over the properties. The "Object.values" method returns an array of the object's property values:

javascriptCopy code

```
const values = Object.values(person); // values contains ["John", "Doe", ...]
```

And the "Object.entries" method returns an array of key-value pairs as arrays:

javascriptCopy code

```
const entries = Object.entries(person); // entries contains [["firstName", "John"], ["lastName", "Doe"], ...]
```

These methods provide different ways to explore and manipulate an object's properties and values. In JavaScript, objects are often used to represent complex data structures and as the building blocks for more advanced features like classes, constructors, and prototypes. Understanding how to work with object properties and methods is essential for developing applications that handle and manipulate data effectively. In summary, objects in JavaScript are versatile data structures that allow you to store and manipulate data using key-value pairs. You can create objects, access their properties and values, add or remove properties, and define methods that operate on the object's data. Understanding these fundamental concepts is crucial for effective JavaScript programming and building robust applications.

Chapter 7: DOM Manipulation and Event Handling

In web development, interacting with the Document Object Model (DOM) is a fundamental part of creating dynamic and interactive web pages. The DOM represents the structured hierarchy of HTML elements in a web page, and JavaScript provides powerful tools for selecting and modifying DOM elements. Being able to manipulate the DOM is essential for building modern web applications and enhancing user interfaces. One of the most common tasks when working with the DOM is selecting HTML elements using JavaScript. You can use various methods and techniques to target specific elements in the DOM so that you can read, modify, or interact with them programmatically. One of the simplest methods to select an element is by using its unique ID attribute. Each HTML element can have an ID attribute, which should be unique within the document. You can select an element by its ID using the getElementById method:

```
javascriptCopy code
const                myElement                =
document.getElementById('uniqueID');
```

In this example, myElement will hold a reference to the HTML element with the specified ID. You can then manipulate this element as needed. If you want to select multiple elements that share the same class name, you can use the getElementsByClassName method:

```
javascriptCopy code
const                elementsWithClass                =
document.getElementsByClassName('commonClass');
```

This method returns a collection of elements that have the specified class. To work with these elements individually, you can access them by their index within the collection. Another way to select elements is by their HTML tag name using the getElementsByTagName method:

javascriptCopy code

```
const allParagraphs = document.getElementsByTagName('p');
```

This method retrieves all the <p> elements in the document and stores them in the allParagraphs collection. Similarly to getElementsByClassName, you can access these elements by their index. If you need to select elements based on more complex criteria or conditions, you can use the querySelector and querySelectorAll methods. The querySelector method allows you to select a single element that matches a CSS selector:

javascriptCopy code

```
const firstButton = document.querySelector('button');
```

In this case, firstButton will reference the first <button> element found in the document. If you want to select multiple elements that match a selector, you can use the querySelectorAll method:

javascriptCopy code

```
const allButtons = document.querySelectorAll('button');
```

allButtons will hold a NodeList containing all the <button> elements in the document. The key advantage of using querySelector and querySelectorAll is the flexibility they offer when specifying the elements to select. You can use complex CSS selectors to target elements based on their attributes, hierarchy, or other characteristics. Once you've

selected DOM elements, you can manipulate them in various ways. For instance, you can change their content by modifying the innerHTML or textContent properties.
javascriptCopy code

```
const            element            =
document.getElementById('myElement');
element.innerHTML = 'New content';
```

In this example, the element with the ID 'myElement' will have its content replaced with 'New content.' Alternatively, you can use the textContent property to change the text content of an element while preserving its HTML structure:
javascriptCopy code

```
const   paragraph   =   document.querySelector('p');
paragraph.textContent = 'This is a new paragraph.';
```

Now, the text content of the selected <p> element has been updated. To change attributes of an element, you can use the setAttribute method:
javascriptCopy code

```
const   link   =   document.querySelector('a');
link.setAttribute('href', 'https://www.example.com');
```

Here, the href attribute of the <a> element has been modified to point to '<u>https://www.example.com</u>.' You can also retrieve attributes using the getAttribute method:
javascriptCopy code

```
const hrefValue = link.getAttribute('href');
```

hrefValue will store the value of the href attribute, which is '<u>https://www.example.com</u>.' In addition to modifying content and attributes, you can change the style of an element by accessing its style property and setting CSS properties:

```javascript
const element = document.querySelector('.styled');
element.style.backgroundColor = 'blue';
element.style.color = 'white';
```

In this example, an element with a class of 'styled' will have its background color set to blue and its text color set to white. CSS properties are camelCased when accessed via JavaScript, such as backgroundColor and color. To add or remove classes from an element, you can use the classList property and its methods:

```javascript
const element = document.querySelector('.toggleClass');
element.classList.add('active');
element.classList.remove('inactive');
```

In this code, the 'active' class is added to the element, while the 'inactive' class is removed. You can also toggle a class on and off using the toggle method:

```javascript
element.classList.toggle('highlight');
```

The classList property is particularly useful for managing CSS classes and applying styles dynamically. When it comes to creating new elements in the DOM, you can use the createElement method:

```javascript
const newDiv = document.createElement('div');
```

This code creates a new <div> element, but it's not yet part of the document. To add it to the DOM, you can use methods like appendChild or insertBefore on a parent element:

```javascript
```

```javascript
const                    parentElement              =
document.querySelector('.container');
parentElement.appendChild(newDiv);
```

Here, the newDiv element is appended to the parentElement, becoming a child element within it. If you need to remove an element from the DOM, you can use the remove method:

javascriptCopy code

```javascript
const                 elementToRemove              =
document.querySelector('.removeMe');
elementToRemove.remove();
```

The remove method completely removes the selected element from the DOM. In addition to modifying individual elements, you can traverse and manipulate the DOM structure itself. For instance, you can access a parent element using the parentNode property:

javascriptCopy code

```javascript
const childElement = document.querySelector('.child');
const parentElement = childElement.parentNode;
```

In this example, parentElement will reference the parent node of childElement. To access the children of an element, you can use the childNodes or children properties:

javascriptCopy code

```javascript
const                 parentElement                =
document.querySelector('.parent'); const childNodes =
parentElement.childNodes;        const    children    =
parentElement.children;
```

childNodes returns all child nodes, including text nodes and whitespace, while children returns only element nodes. To navigate to siblings, you can use properties like nextSibling and previousSibling:

javascriptCopy code

```
const currentElement = document.querySelector('.current'); const nextElement = currentElement.nextSibling; const previousElement = currentElement.previousSibling;
```

These properties give you access to the adjacent sibling nodes of an element. When dealing with events, you can use JavaScript to add event listeners to DOM elements. Event listeners allow you to respond to user interactions such as clicks, mouse movements, and keyboard input. Here's an example of adding a click event listener to a button element:

javascriptCopy code

```
const button = document.querySelector('button'); button.addEventListener('click', function () { console.log('Button clicked!'); });
```

In this code, when the button is clicked, the provided function is executed, logging 'Button clicked!' to the console. You can also remove event listeners using the removeEventListener method, passing in the same function reference:

javascriptCopy code

```
function clickHandler() { console.log('Button clicked!'); } button.addEventListener('click', clickHandler); // Later, remove the event listener button.removeEventListener('click', clickHandler);
```

This ensures that the event listener is no longer active and won't trigger the specified function when the event occurs. In summary, working with the DOM in JavaScript involves selecting elements, modifying their content and attributes, and responding to user interactions. You can select elements by ID, class, tag name, or using complex CSS selectors with methods like getElementById, getElementsByClassName, getElementsByTagName, querySelector, and querySelectorAll. Once you have references to elements, you can manipulate their content, attributes, styles, and classes using various properties and methods. Additionally, you can create new elements, append or remove them from the DOM, and traverse the DOM structure. Event listeners play a crucial role in making web pages interactive by allowing you to respond to user actions, such as clicks and keystrokes. Understanding how to select and modify DOM elements is a fundamental skill for web developers, enabling them to create dynamic and engaging web applications.

In web development, providing interactivity and responsiveness to user actions is a crucial aspect of creating engaging and dynamic web applications. To achieve this, JavaScript offers powerful capabilities for handling user events. User events can be triggered by various actions, such as clicking a button, moving the mouse, typing on the keyboard, or resizing the browser window. Handling these events allows you to respond to user input and create interactive experiences. One of the most common user events is the "click" event, which occurs when a user clicks on an HTML element, such as a button, link, or image. To handle a click event, you can attach an event listener to the target element using JavaScript. Here's an example of adding a click event listener to a button element:

javascriptCopy code

```javascript
const button = document.querySelector('button');
button.addEventListener('click', function () { // Code to execute when the button is clicked });
```

In this code, when the button is clicked, the function provided as the second argument to addEventListener will be executed. You can use this function to define the behavior or action you want to perform in response to the click event. For example, you can update the content of an HTML element:

javascriptCopy code

```javascript
const button = document.querySelector('button'); const outputElement = document.querySelector('#output');
button.addEventListener('click', function () { outputElement.textContent = 'Button clicked!'; });
```

In this case, when the button is clicked, the text content of the element with the ID 'output' is changed to 'Button clicked!'. Besides the "click" event, there are numerous other events that you can listen for, including "mouseover," "mouseout," "keydown," "keyup," "mousemove," and many more. For keyboard-related events, you can capture keycodes to respond to specific keys. For example, you can listen for the "keydown" event and check if the pressed key is the Enter key:

javascriptCopy code

```javascript
const inputElement = document.querySelector('input');
inputElement.addEventListener('keydown', function (event) { if (event.key === 'Enter') { // Code to execute when Enter key is pressed } });
```

By examining the event object passed to the event handler, you can access information about the event, such as the key pressed or the mouse coordinates. To prevent the default behavior of an event, you can call the preventDefault method on the event object. For instance, you can prevent a form from being submitted when the Enter key is pressed:

javascriptCopy code

```
const formElement = document.querySelector('form');
formElement.addEventListener('submit', function (event) { event.preventDefault(); // Prevent the default form submission // Code to handle the form data });
```

This prevents the default browser behavior of submitting the form and allows you to handle the form data using your custom logic. In addition to handling single events, you can use event delegation to manage events for multiple elements efficiently. Event delegation involves attaching a single event listener to a common ancestor of several elements you want to target. For example, if you have a list of items and want to handle click events on each item, you can add a single event listener to the parent list element:

javascriptCopy code

```
const listElement = document.querySelector('ul');
listElement.addEventListener('click', function (event) { if (event.target.tagName === 'LI') { // Code to execute when a list item is clicked } });
```

With event delegation, you can determine which specific child element triggered the event and respond accordingly. This approach is particularly useful when dealing with dynamically generated content or large lists of items. Another important aspect of handling user events is asynchronous operations, such as fetching data from a server using AJAX or making network requests. JavaScript provides tools for making asynchronous calls, such as the XMLHttpRequest object or the more modern fetch API. When working with asynchronous operations, it's essential to handle events like "load," "error," and "readystatechange" to manage the request's lifecycle and handle responses or errors appropriately. For example, when using the fetch API to retrieve data from a remote server, you can handle the promise returned by the fetch function:

javascriptCopy code

```javascript
fetch('https://api.example.com/data').then(response => { if (!response.ok) { throw new Error('Network response was not ok'); } return response.json(); })
.then(data => { // Code to handle the retrieved data })
.catch(error => { // Code to handle errors });
```

In this code, the .then() method is used to handle the response and parse the JSON data, while the .catch() method handles any errors that may occur during the request. Asynchronous event handling allows you to create responsive web applications that can update content without requiring a full page reload. Another common use case for event handling is form validation. You can use event listeners to validate user input in real-time and provide feedback to users as they fill out forms. For example, you can listen for the "input" event on an input field to validate its value as the user types:

javascriptCopy code

```
const inputElement = document.querySelector('input');
inputElement.addEventListener('input', function () {
const inputValue = inputElement.value; if
(inputValue.length < 5) { // Display an error message or
change the input style } else { // Hide the error message
or reset the input style } });
```

This code checks the length of the input value and provides immediate feedback to the user based on the validation rules. Handling user events and interactivity is a fundamental part of web development, enabling you to create responsive and engaging web applications. Whether it's responding to clicks, key presses, or asynchronous data fetching, JavaScript's event handling capabilities empower developers to create dynamic and interactive user experiences. By leveraging event listeners and event delegation, you can build web applications that respond to user input effectively and provide a smooth and engaging user interface.

Chapter 8: Asynchronous Programming with Promises

In the world of web development, the term "asynchronous code" plays a pivotal role in creating responsive and efficient web applications. As the web has evolved, user expectations for seamless experiences have grown, and asynchronous programming has become an essential technique to meet these expectations. At its core, asynchronous code allows you to perform tasks concurrently, without blocking the execution of other code. This is particularly crucial when dealing with time-consuming operations, such as network requests, file reading, or database queries. To understand asynchronous code, it's essential to first grasp the concept of synchronous code. Synchronous code, also known as blocking code, executes one operation at a time, in a sequential manner. When a function or operation is called in synchronous code, it must complete before the program can proceed to the next line of code. Consider a simple example of synchronous code:

```javascript
javascriptCopy code
function greet(name) { return "Hello, " + name + "!";
} const message = greet("Alice");
console.log(message);
```

In this synchronous code, the greet function is called with the argument "Alice." The function computes the greeting message and returns it, which is then assigned to the message variable. Finally, the message is logged to the console. This entire process happens sequentially, one step after another, from top to bottom. While this works well for many tasks, it becomes problematic when dealing with operations that take time, like fetching data from an external server. In synchronous code, if a function performs a time-consuming task, it can block the entire program until it completes. For example, if you're making a network request to fetch data, the browser would be unresponsive until the request finishes. This is where asynchronous code comes to the rescue. Asynchronous code allows you to initiate a task and continue with other operations without waiting for the task to complete. Instead of blocking the program, asynchronous operations run in the background, and you can specify what should happen once they finish. JavaScript provides several mechanisms for writing asynchronous code, such as callbacks, Promises, and async/await. Callbacks were one of the earliest ways to handle asynchronous code in JavaScript. A callback is a function that you pass as an argument to another function, and it gets executed when the asynchronous operation is complete. Here's an example of using callbacks for an asynchronous operation, like reading a file:

javascriptCopy code

```
function readFile(callback) { setTimeout(function () {
const content = "This is the file content.";
callback(content); }, 1000); } readFile(function
```

(content) { console.log("File content: " + content); });
console.log("Reading file...");
In this example, the readFile function simulates reading a file asynchronously using setTimeout. When the file read operation is complete, it calls the provided callback function with the file's content. Meanwhile, the program continues executing other code. When the asynchronous operation finishes, the callback function is invoked, and the file content is logged to the console. Callbacks are effective for handling asynchronous code but can lead to a nesting pattern known as "callback hell" or "pyramid of doom" when dealing with multiple asynchronous operations. Promises were introduced to address this issue and provide a more structured way to handle asynchronous code. A Promise is an object representing the eventual completion or failure of an asynchronous operation. It has three states: pending, fulfilled, or rejected. Here's an example of using Promises for the same file reading operation:
javascriptCopy code

```
function readFile() { return new Promise(function
(resolve, reject) { setTimeout(function () { const
content = "This is the file content."; resolve(content);
}, 1000); }); } readFile() .then(function (content) {
console.log("File content: " + content); })
.catch(function (error) { console.error("Error: " +
error); }); console.log("Reading file...");
```

In this code, the readFile function returns a Promise. Inside the Promise constructor, the asynchronous operation is performed, and resolve is called when it's successful, while reject is used for errors. Using the .then() method, you can specify what should happen when the Promise is fulfilled, and the .catch() method handles errors. Promises provide a more structured and readable way to handle asynchronous code, making it easier to manage complex sequences of asynchronous operations. Async/await is a more recent addition to JavaScript, building on top of Promises to make asynchronous code even more readable and maintainable. With async/await, you can write asynchronous code that looks almost like synchronous code. Here's how the previous file reading example can be rewritten using async/await:

javascriptCopy code

```
async function readFile() { return new
Promise(function (resolve) { setTimeout(function () {
const content = "This is the file content.";
resolve(content); }, 1000); }); } async function main() {
try { const content = await readFile();
console.log("File content: " + content); } catch (error)
{ console.error("Error: " + error); } } main();
console.log("Reading file...");
```

In this code, the readFile function is marked as async, indicating that it returns a Promise. Inside the main function, await is used to pause execution until the Promise is resolved. This makes the code read like a series of synchronous operations, making it easier to understand and maintain. Async/await has become the preferred way to handle asynchronous code in modern JavaScript development. Asynchronous code is not limited to I/O operations; it also plays a crucial role in handling user interactions in web applications. For example, when a user clicks a button to submit a form, the form submission should not block the user interface. Instead, the submission should happen asynchronously in the background while the user can continue interacting with the page. To achieve this, you can attach an event listener to the form's submit event and prevent the default behavior, which would cause a page reload.

javascriptCopy code

```
const form = document.querySelector('form');
form.addEventListener('submit', async function (event) { event.preventDefault(); // Prevent the default form submission try { const response = await fetch('https://api.example.com/submit', { method: 'POST', body: new FormData(form), }); if (response.ok) { console.log('Form submitted successfully.'); } else { console.error('Form submission failed.'); } } catch (error) { console.error('An error occurred:', error); } });
```

In this code, the form submission is handled asynchronously using the fetch API with async/await. By handling user interactions asynchronously, you ensure that the web application remains responsive and provides a smoother user experience. In summary, asynchronous code is a fundamental concept in web development, allowing you to perform time-consuming operations without blocking the execution of other code. JavaScript provides various mechanisms for writing asynchronous code, including callbacks, Promises, and async/await. These techniques enable you to handle events, make network requests, and manage user interactions seamlessly, creating responsive and efficient web applications that meet the expectations of today's users.

In the world of asynchronous JavaScript, Promises serve as a powerful tool not only for managing the flow of data but also for handling errors gracefully. When working with asynchronous operations, errors are an inevitable part of the process, and how you handle them can significantly impact the reliability and robustness of your code. Promises provide a structured approach to error handling, allowing you to catch and handle errors in a clean and consistent manner. Let's explore how Promises can be used for error handling and chaining in asynchronous JavaScript code. One of the key features of Promises is their ability to handle both successful and failed outcomes of asynchronous operations. When a Promise is resolved successfully, it enters the "fulfilled" state, and you can execute specific code to handle the successful result. However, when an error occurs during the execution of the asynchronous operation, the Promise enters the "rejected" state, and you can gracefully handle the error. Here's a basic example of a Promise that simulates a successful and failed asynchronous operation:
javascriptCopy code
const successfulPromise = new Promise((resolve, reject) => { setTimeout(() => { resolve('Operation

```
succeeded'); }, 1000); }); const failedPromise = new
Promise((resolve, reject) => { setTimeout(() => {
reject(new Error('Operation failed')); }, 1000); });
successfulPromise        .then((result)        =>        {
console.log('Success:', result); }) .catch((error) => {
console.error('Error:',   error);   });   failedPromise
.then((result) => { console.log('Success:', result); })
.catch((error) => { console.error('Error:', error); });
```

In this example, successfulPromise resolves successfully after a delay, while failedPromise is explicitly rejected with an error. When working with Promises, you can use the .then() method to specify what should happen when the Promise is fulfilled successfully. Likewise, you can use the .catch() method to define how to handle errors when the Promise is rejected. This separation of success and error handling makes your code more readable and maintainable. Promises also allow you to chain multiple asynchronous operations together, which is a common requirement in many applications. Chaining Promises ensures that one operation completes before the next one starts, maintaining a clear and organized flow of execution. Consider a scenario where you need to fetch data from a server, process it, and then save it to a database. Chaining Promises simplifies this process by ensuring that each step is executed in sequence. Here's an example of chaining Promises for this scenario:

javascriptCopy code

```
function fetchData() { return new Promise((resolve,
reject) => { // Simulate fetching data from a server
setTimeout(() => { const data = { id: 1, name: 'John'
}; resolve(data); }, 1000); }); } function
processAndSaveData(data) { return new
Promise((resolve, reject) => { // Simulate processing
and saving data setTimeout(() => { data.processed =
true; resolve(data); }, 1000); }); } fetchData()
.then(processAndSaveData) .then((result) => {
console.log('Data processed and saved:', result); })
.catch((error) => { console.error('Error:', error); });
```

In this code, the fetchData function fetches data from a
server and resolves with the fetched data. The
processAndSaveData function processes the data and
resolves with the processed data. By chaining the two
Promises using .then(), you ensure that the data is
processed and saved only after it has been successfully
fetched. If any step in the chain encounters an error,
the .catch() block is executed to handle the error
gracefully. This error-handling mechanism simplifies the
management of asynchronous workflows and ensures
that any errors are properly captured and addressed.
Promises also provide a way to perform parallel
asynchronous operations and handle their results when
they all complete. This is achieved using Promise.all(),
which takes an array of Promises and returns a new
Promise that fulfills with an array of results when all the
input Promises are fulfilled successfully. If any of the
input Promises are rejected, the resulting Promise is

also rejected. Here's an example of using Promise.all() to fetch data from multiple sources in parallel:
javascriptCopy code

```
const fetchUserData = new Promise((resolve, reject) => { setTimeout(() => { resolve({ id: 1, name: 'Alice' }); }, 1000); }); const fetchPostData = new Promise((resolve, reject) => { setTimeout(() => { resolve({ userId: 1, title: 'Post 1' }); }, 1500); }); const fetchCommentData = new Promise((resolve, reject) => { setTimeout(() => { resolve({ postId: 1, text: 'Comment on Post 1' }); }, 2000); }); Promise.all([fetchUserData, fetchPostData, fetchCommentData]) .then((results) => { const [userData, postData, commentData] = results; console.log('User:', userData); console.log('Post:', postData); console.log('Comment:', commentData); }) .catch((error) => { console.error('Error:', error); });
```

In this example, three Promises fetch user data, post data, and comment data simultaneously. Promise.all() is used to wait for all three Promises to complete and collect their results in an array. If all Promises fulfill successfully, the .then() block processes and logs the collected data. If any of the Promises reject, the .catch() block handles the error. This ensures that all asynchronous operations are coordinated, and you can proceed with processing the results when they are all available. Promises provide a clear and structured way to handle errors and orchestrate complex asynchronous workflows in JavaScript. They offer a clean separation between success and error handling through the use of .then() and .catch() methods. Chaining Promises allows you to create a sequential flow of asynchronous operations, ensuring that each step is executed in order. Additionally, Promise.all() simplifies the parallel execution of asynchronous tasks and allows you to handle their results collectively. By mastering the use of Promises for error handling and chaining, you can write more robust and maintainable asynchronous code in your JavaScript applications.

Chapter 9: Form Validation and User Interaction

In web development, forms are a fundamental part of user interaction, enabling users to submit data to websites and applications. However, ensuring that the data submitted through forms is valid and secure is essential for maintaining the integrity of your application. To achieve this, form input validation is a critical step in the process, allowing you to check and sanitize user input before it is processed or stored. Next, we'll explore the principles and techniques of validating form input in JavaScript.

Form input validation involves verifying that the data entered by the user conforms to specific criteria, such as required fields, data types, and acceptable values. By enforcing these criteria, you can prevent erroneous or malicious data from entering your system, enhancing both the reliability and security of your application. One of the most common types of form validation is ensuring that required fields are filled out. This involves checking that essential information, such as email addresses, passwords, or shipping addresses, is provided by the user. In JavaScript, you can access form elements using the Document Object Model (DOM), allowing you to examine their values and attributes. For instance, to check if a text input field with the id "email" is empty, you can use the following code:

javascriptCopy code

```javascript
const emailField = document.getElementById('email');
const emailValue = emailField.value; if (emailValue
=== '') { // Display an error message or take
appropriate action }
```

In this code, we first obtain a reference to the input field with the id "email" and then retrieve its current value. We can then check if the value is an empty string, indicating that the user has not entered any text.

Another essential aspect of form validation is validating data types. For example, when users are asked to provide their age, you want to ensure that they enter a valid number. JavaScript provides functions like isNaN() to check if a value is not a number and parseInt() to parse integers from strings. Here's an example of validating a user's age:

javascriptCopy code

```javascript
const ageField = document.getElementById('age');
const ageValue = ageField.value; const age =
parseInt(ageValue); if (isNaN(age)) { // Display an
error message or take appropriate action }
```

In this code, we first obtain the age input field's value and attempt to parse it as an integer. If the parsing fails, indicating that the value is not a valid number, we can display an error message or take appropriate action.

In addition to validating data types, you may need to ensure that certain input adheres to specific patterns or formats. For instance, you can validate email addresses, phone numbers, or postal codes using regular expressions. Regular expressions provide a powerful and flexible way to define patterns for matching and validating text. Here's an example of validating an email address:

javascriptCopy code

```
const emailField = document.getElementById('email');
const emailValue = emailField.value; const emailPattern = /^[a-zA-Z0-9._-]+@[a-zA-Z0-9.-]+\.[a-zA-Z]{2,4}$/; if (!emailPattern.test(emailValue)) { // Display an error message or take appropriate action }
```

In this code, we define a regular expression pattern for validating email addresses. We then use the test() method to check if the email value matches the pattern. If it doesn't, we can display an error message or take the necessary steps.

Form validation often involves providing informative feedback to users when errors occur. This feedback can take the form of error messages, visual cues, or suggestions for correcting input. By providing clear and helpful feedback, you enhance the user experience and assist users in completing forms correctly.

When it comes to displaying error messages, you can dynamically create elements to hold the messages and insert them into the DOM. For example, you can create a <div> element for displaying an error message and append it to a specific location on the page:

javascriptCopy code

```
const errorDiv = document.createElement('div');
errorDiv.textContent = 'Please enter a valid email address.'; errorDiv.className = 'error-message'; const
```

```
emailField    =    document.getElementById('email');
emailField.parentNode.appendChild(errorDiv);
```

In this code, we create a new <div> element, set its text content to the error message, assign a class for styling, and then append it to the parent element of the email input field. This places the error message in a visible location on the page.

In addition to displaying error messages, you can visually indicate invalid input by changing the style or color of the form elements. For example, you can apply a red border to an invalid input field to draw the user's attention:

javascriptCopy code

```
const emailField = document.getElementById('email');
const emailValue = emailField.value; const
emailPattern = /^[a-zA-Z0-9._-]+@[a-zA-Z0-9.-]+\.[a-zA-
Z]{2,4}$/; if (!emailPattern.test(emailValue)) {
emailField.classList.add('invalid-input'); } else {
emailField.classList.remove('invalid-input'); }
```

In this code, we use the classList property to add or remove the "invalid-input" class based on whether the email value matches the pattern. You can define CSS styles to apply specific visual changes when the "invalid-input" class is present.

To assist users in correcting their input, you can provide helpful hints or suggestions alongside form fields. For instance, you can add placeholder text inside an input field to give users an idea of the expected format or content.

htmlCopy code

```
<input type="text" id="email" placeholder="Enter your
email address">
```
In this example, the "Enter your email address" placeholder text provides guidance to users about the expected input.

In modern web development, client-side form validation in JavaScript is often complemented by server-side validation. Client-side validation focuses on providing immediate feedback to users and enhancing the user experience, while server-side validation ensures the security and integrity of the data submitted to the server. Server-side validation is essential because client-side validation can be bypassed or manipulated by malicious users. For example, a user with knowledge of JavaScript can disable client-side validation or submit custom data. Server-side validation acts as the last line of defense, ensuring that only valid and secure data is processed and stored.

When implementing server-side validation, you should revalidate the data submitted by the user, regardless of the client-side validation. This redundancy ensures that any potential vulnerabilities or errors in the client-side code do not compromise the security of your application. Server-side validation can check for issues such as data integrity, data length, data format, and data consistency. It can also prevent common security threats like SQL injection and cross-site scripting (XSS) attacks.

In summary, form input validation is a crucial part of web development, ensuring that data submitted by users is accurate, secure, and reliable. JavaScript plays a central role in client-side validation, allowing you to check required fields, validate data types, and enforce specific patterns. Providing clear error messages, visual cues, and helpful hints enhances the user experience and encourages correct input. However, server-side validation remains essential for data security and integrity, acting as a safeguard against potential vulnerabilities and malicious attacks. By combining client-side and server-side validation, you can create robust and secure web applications that offer a seamless user experience.

In the realm of web development, providing an exceptional user experience is paramount to the success of any application or website. One of the fundamental ways to achieve this is by enhancing interactivity through event listeners. Event listeners are JavaScript mechanisms that allow you to respond to user actions and interactions, making your web pages dynamic and engaging. Next, we'll delve into the world of event listeners and discover how they can elevate the user experience.

At its core, an event listener is a JavaScript function that "listens" for a specific event to occur and then executes a set of instructions in response. Events can encompass a wide range of user interactions, such as clicks, keyboard inputs, mouse movements, form submissions, and more. By attaching event listeners to HTML elements, you can dictate how your web page should react when users interact with those elements.

The process of adding an event listener to an HTML element typically involves three steps. First, you select the HTML element you want to target. This can be done using JavaScript's Document Object Model (DOM) API, which provides methods to access and manipulate HTML elements. For example, you can use the getElementById() method to select an element by its unique ID or querySelector() to target elements by CSS selectors.

Next, you specify the type of event you want to listen for. This could be something like a "click" event for a button, a "submit" event for a form, or a "keydown" event for a specific keyboard key. Each type of event corresponds to a particular user action or system event.

Finally, you define the function that should be executed when the event occurs. This function, known as the event handler or callback, contains the code that responds to the event. It can perform a wide range of actions, such as changing the content of the page, displaying a message, or triggering animations.

Here's an example of attaching a click event listener to a button element:

javascriptCopy code

```
const myButton = document.getElementById('my-button');           myButton.addEventListener('click',
function() { // Code to be executed when the button is clicked });
```

In this code, we first select the button element with the ID "my-button" using getElementById(). Next, we attach a click event listener to the button using the addEventListener() method. When the button is clicked, the anonymous function provided as the second argument will be executed.

Event listeners can also be used to handle keyboard interactions. For instance, you can listen for the "keydown" event on a specific key, such as the Enter key, to trigger an action when the user presses it.

javascriptCopy code

```
document.addEventListener('keydown',
function(event) { if (event.key === 'Enter') { // Code
to be executed when the Enter key is pressed } });
```

In this example, we add a "keydown" event listener to the entire document and check if the pressed key is the Enter key inside the event handler.

Another valuable use of event listeners is in form validation. When a user submits a form, you can prevent the default form submission behavior and instead validate the input data using event listeners.

javascriptCopy code

```
const myForm = document.getElementById('my-
form'); myForm.addEventListener('submit',
function(event) { event.preventDefault(); // Prevent
the form from submitting // Code to validate form
input and provide feedback to the user });
```

By calling event.preventDefault(), we stop the default form submission behavior and can implement custom validation logic inside the event handler.

Event listeners also enable you to create interactive elements, such as dropdown menus, accordions, and modal dialogs. These components can be hidden or displayed in response to user interactions, providing a smoother and more engaging user experience.

For example, you can create a simple dropdown menu that appears when a button is clicked:

javascriptCopy code

```
const dropdownButton = document.getElementById('dropdown-button'); const dropdownMenu = document.getElementById('dropdown-menu');
dropdownButton.addEventListener('click', function() { dropdownMenu.classList.toggle('visible'); });
```

In this code, the click event listener toggles the "visible" class on the dropdown menu, making it appear and disappear when the button is clicked.

Event listeners also play a significant role in handling asynchronous operations and fetching data from external sources. When making network requests using techniques like the Fetch API or XMLHttpRequest, you can use event listeners to respond to the completion of the request and process the retrieved data.

javascriptCopy code

```
const fetchDataButton = document.getElementById('fetch-data-button'); const dataContainer = document.getElementById('data-container'); fetchDataButton.addEventListener('click', function() { fetch('https://api.example.com/data') .then(response => response.json()) .then(data => { // Code to display the fetched data in the data container dataContainer.textContent = JSON.stringify(data,
```

null, 2); }) .catch(error => { console.error('Error:', error); }); });

In this example, clicking the "Fetch Data" button triggers a network request to retrieve data from an API. The event listener handles the response, parses the JSON data, and displays it in the "data-container" element.

One of the key advantages of event listeners is their ability to support multiple listeners for the same event on a single element. This means that you can attach multiple event listeners to an element, and all of them will be executed when the event occurs. This feature allows you to modularize your code and separate concerns by having different listeners perform specific tasks.

For example, you can have one listener responsible for handling the visual aspect of an interaction, such as changing the color of a button when it's clicked, and another listener for performing a functional task, such as submitting a form.

javascriptCopy code

```
const myButton = document.getElementById('my-button');
myButton.addEventListener('click', function() { // Code for visual interaction (e.g., change button color) });
myButton.addEventListener('click', function() { // Code for functional task (e.g., form submission) });
```

In this code, both event listeners are attached to the same button, and they will be executed in the order they were added.

Event delegation is another advanced concept that leverages event listeners to handle events for multiple elements efficiently. Instead of attaching individual event listeners to each element, you can attach a single event listener to a common ancestor element and use event delegation to determine which specific element triggered the event. This technique is particularly useful for elements that are dynamically generated or frequently updated.

In summary, event listeners are a foundational tool in web development for enhancing user experience and interactivity. They enable you to respond to a wide range of user actions and interactions, from simple clicks and keyboard inputs to complex interactions like form submissions and network requests. By effectively using event listeners, you can create dynamic and engaging web pages that provide users with a seamless and interactive experience, making your web applications more user-friendly and compelling.

Chapter 10: Introduction to Debugging and Troubleshooting

In the world of programming, encountering errors is an inevitable part of the journey, and JavaScript is no exception. Whether you're a novice or an experienced developer, dealing with errors is a crucial skill. Next, we'll explore some common JavaScript errors and provide solutions to help you diagnose and rectify them. One of the most basic and frequent errors in JavaScript is the "SyntaxError." This error occurs when the JavaScript engine encounters code that violates the language's syntax rules. Common causes of SyntaxErrors include missing parentheses, semicolons, or curly braces. To resolve SyntaxErrors, carefully review your code and ensure that all syntax rules are followed. A good practice is to use a code editor or Integrated Development Environment (IDE) that highlights syntax errors in real-time.

Another common error is the "ReferenceError." This error arises when you attempt to access a variable or function that is not defined. To solve ReferenceErrors, check for typographical errors in variable or function names and ensure that they are declared and in scope at the point of use. If a variable is supposed to be global, make sure it's not accidentally enclosed within a local scope.

The "TypeError" is a frequent error caused by attempting to perform an operation on a value of an inappropriate type. For instance, trying to call a method on a non-function or access a property of an undefined or null value can result in a TypeError. To tackle TypeErrors, double-check the types of your variables and values and ensure that they match the expected types for the operations you're performing. You can use conditional statements or type-checking functions like typeof to validate types before executing code.

The "RangeError" is thrown when an operation exceeds the allowed range of values. For example, attempting to create an array with an excessively large length or recursively calling a function without a base case can lead to a RangeError. To overcome RangeErrors, review your code to ensure that you're not pushing limits beyond the JavaScript engine's capabilities. Consider using iterative solutions for tasks that could trigger stack overflow errors.

One error that often occurs when working with asynchronous operations is the "Callback Hell" or "Pyramid of Doom." This error manifests as deeply nested callback functions, making the code hard to read and maintain. To mitigate callback hell, employ techniques like modularization, named functions, and Promises. Breaking down complex asynchronous operations into smaller, reusable functions can significantly improve code readability and maintainability.

A special type of error that can be challenging to debug is the "Null or Undefined Value." These errors occur when you attempt to access properties or methods of values that are null or undefined. To handle null or undefined values, use conditional statements or optional chaining (available in modern JavaScript) to gracefully check and handle these cases.

"Variable Hoisting" is a behavior in JavaScript where variable declarations are moved to the top of their containing function or block scope during compilation. This can lead to unexpected results if you're not aware of how hoisting works. To avoid hoisting-related issues, declare your variables at the top of their respective scopes and initialize them before use.

"NaN" (Not-a-Number) is a special value in JavaScript that represents the result of an invalid mathematical operation. It can be problematic when it propagates through calculations. To prevent NaN issues, validate input values before performing mathematical operations, and use functions like isNaN() or Number.isNaN() to check for NaN values explicitly.

"Cross-Origin Resource Sharing (CORS) Errors" occur when you attempt to make AJAX requests to a different domain from the one hosting your JavaScript code. To resolve CORS errors, you must configure the server to include the appropriate CORS headers, allowing requests from your domain.

When working with asynchronous code, timing issues can lead to "Race Conditions" or "Callback Timing Errors." These occur when you expect one asynchronous operation to complete before another but can't guarantee the order of execution. To handle race conditions, use mechanisms like Promises, async/await, or callback sequencing to ensure that asynchronous operations occur in the desired order.

"Memory Leaks" can be a subtle yet severe issue in JavaScript applications. These occur when objects are unintentionally kept in memory, preventing them from being garbage collected. To prevent memory leaks, pay close attention to event listeners and object references. Remove event listeners when they are no longer needed and release references to objects that are no longer in use.

Another type of error related to asynchronous code is the "Callback Reference Error." This occurs when a callback function references variables that have gone out of scope by the time the callback is executed. To avoid this error, use closures or pass necessary variables as function arguments to ensure they remain in scope when needed.

"Unhandled Promise Rejections" are errors that arise when a Promise is rejected but no .catch() or await handles the rejection. To address unhandled promise rejections, always handle Promise rejections with .catch() or try...catch blocks when working with async code.

"Web API Errors" can occur when using browser-specific APIs. For example, attempting to access a non-existent DOM element can result in an error. To prevent such errors, verify that the elements you're trying to access exist before interacting with them.

In summary, encountering errors is an intrinsic part of JavaScript development. However, understanding common error types and their solutions can help you become a more proficient developer. Regularly debugging your code, utilizing development tools, and writing tests can also assist in identifying and resolving errors efficiently. By mastering the art of handling errors, you'll not only improve your coding skills but also build more robust and reliable JavaScript applications.

Debugging is an indispensable skill for every web developer, and when it comes to JavaScript debugging, browser developer tools are your best ally. These tools provide a comprehensive set of features and capabilities for inspecting, analyzing, and troubleshooting your web applications. Next, we'll explore how to effectively use browser developer tools to debug JavaScript code and solve common issues.

Most modern web browsers come equipped with robust developer tools. To access them, simply right-click anywhere on a web page and select "Inspect" or press the F12 key (or Ctrl+Shift+I on Windows, or Command+Option+I on macOS). This action will open the developer tools panel, which typically appears at the bottom or right side of your browser window.

One of the fundamental features of browser developer tools is the "Elements" panel. This panel allows you to inspect and manipulate the Document Object Model (DOM) of a web page. You can hover over HTML elements in the "Elements" panel to highlight corresponding elements on the page, making it easier to identify and select specific elements. You can also edit HTML and CSS in real-time, enabling rapid prototyping and testing of design changes.

The "Console" panel is where you'll spend a significant portion of your time when debugging JavaScript. It provides an interactive JavaScript console where you can execute code, log messages, and catch errors. You can type JavaScript expressions directly into the console and see the results instantly. This feature is invaluable for experimenting with code snippets and testing hypotheses quickly.

When an error occurs in your JavaScript code, the "Console" panel is your first stop for debugging. Error messages are displayed here, along with information about the error type, stack trace, and the file and line number where the error occurred. Clicking on the error message will often take you directly to the relevant line of code in the "Sources" panel, helping you pinpoint the issue.

The "Sources" panel is where you can examine and debug your JavaScript source code. Here, you'll find a file navigator on the left, displaying all the scripts associated with the web page. You can expand and collapse folders to organize your scripts effectively. To debug a specific JavaScript file, click on it in the navigator to open it in the editor.

Once you have a JavaScript file open in the "Sources" panel, you can set breakpoints to pause the execution of your code at specific lines. To set a breakpoint, click on the line number where you want execution to pause. When you interact with your web page and trigger the code containing the breakpoint, execution will halt, and the "Call Stack" and "Variables" panels will become active.

The "Call Stack" panel shows you the sequence of function calls that led to the current point in your code.

You can inspect the stack to understand the flow of execution and how you arrived at the current state. Clicking on a function in the stack will take you to the corresponding line of code, making it easier to trace the error's origin.

The "Variables" panel provides a detailed view of the variables and their values at the current point in your code. You can add variables to the watchlist for quick reference and monitor their values as you step through your code. Stepping through code is possible with the "Step Into," "Step Over," and "Step Out" buttons in the toolbar, allowing you to navigate through function calls and loops.

Conditional breakpoints are another powerful feature of the "Sources" panel. You can set breakpoints with conditions based on expressions, ensuring that the code pauses only when specific criteria are met. This capability is handy when you want to isolate issues that occur under certain conditions, such as when a variable reaches a particular value.

The "Network" panel is indispensable for debugging issues related to network requests. It allows you to monitor and inspect HTTP requests and responses, including headers, payloads, and timing information. You can filter and search for requests, simulate different network conditions (e.g., slow 3G or offline), and analyze performance bottlenecks.

When dealing with asynchronous code, the "Timeline" and "Performance" panels can be incredibly helpful. The "Timeline" panel records and visualizes events, such as JavaScript execution, rendering, and network activity.

You can use it to identify performance bottlenecks and analyze how your web page loads and responds to user interactions. The "Performance" panel provides even more in-depth performance analysis, including CPU and memory profiling.

Another essential tool for debugging JavaScript is the "Application" panel. Here, you can inspect and manipulate web storage (localStorage and sessionStorage), cookies, and service workers. You can clear storage, modify values, and simulate different scenarios to test how your web application behaves under various conditions.

The "Security" panel is useful for checking the security of your web page. It provides information about SSL/TLS certificates, mixed content issues, and insecure resources. You can also use it to analyze security-related headers sent by the server.

Browser developer tools offer a wealth of additional features and extensions that can enhance your debugging workflow. For example, you can install browser extensions like "React DevTools" for debugging React applications or "Vue.js Devtools" for Vue.js applications. These extensions provide specialized panels for debugging specific JavaScript libraries and frameworks.

Additionally, some browser developer tools support live editing and debugging of CSS with the "Styles" panel. You can experiment with CSS changes, view computed styles, and identify the source of specific styles applied to elements.

Browser developer tools are not limited to just debugging JavaScript and inspecting the DOM. They can also help you audit your web page for accessibility issues, performance optimizations, and mobile responsiveness. These audits provide valuable insights and recommendations for improving the quality and performance of your web applications.

In summary, browser developer tools are an essential part of a web developer's toolkit. They empower you to inspect, debug, and optimize your JavaScript code, ensuring that your web applications run smoothly and efficiently. By mastering these tools and their features, you can become a more effective developer, capable of tackling complex issues and delivering high-quality web experiences to users.

BOOK 2
INTERMEDIATE JAVASCRIPT MASTERY BUILDING WEB APPLICATIONS WITH ES6 AND BEYOND

ROB BOTWRIGHT

Chapter 1: Recap of JavaScript Fundamentals

In the realm of JavaScript programming, variables serve as the building blocks of your code, allowing you to store and manipulate data. Variables are like containers that hold information, such as numbers, text, and more. Understanding how to work with variables, data types, and operators is fundamental to mastering JavaScript. At its core, a variable is a symbolic name that references a value in memory. You can think of a variable as a label you attach to data, making it easier to manage and manipulate that data in your code. In JavaScript, you declare variables using keywords like var, let, or const.

The var keyword was historically used to declare variables, but it has some quirks and scope-related issues. It's best to avoid var in modern JavaScript development. Instead, prefer let and const. The let keyword allows you to declare mutable variables, which means their values can be changed after initial assignment. On the other hand, the const keyword is used for declaring variables whose values should not be reassigned once set. Using const can lead to more predictable and error-resistant code.

JavaScript offers several built-in data types, each designed to store different kinds of information. The most basic data types are "primitive" types, which include numbers, strings, booleans, null, undefined, and symbols. Numbers can represent both integers and floating-point values, making them versatile for mathematical operations. Strings are sequences of characters and are used for representing text. Booleans can be either true or false and are used for logical conditions. Null represents the intentional absence of any value, while undefined is used to denote uninitialized variables. Symbols are unique and are often used for creating private object properties.

In JavaScript, you don't need to declare the data type of a variable explicitly. The language employs "dynamic typing," which means the data type of a variable is determined at runtime based on the assigned value. For example, you can assign a number to a variable, and later, without error, assign a string to the same variable.

Operators in JavaScript are used to perform operations on variables and values. There are several types of operators, including arithmetic, comparison, logical, assignment, and more. Arithmetic operators allow you to perform mathematical calculations, such as addition, subtraction, multiplication, and division. Comparison operators are used to compare values and return a boolean result, indicating whether a condition is true or false. Logical operators are used to perform logical operations, such as AND (&&) and OR (||), which are often used in conditional statements. Assignment operators are used to assign values to variables, and there are shorthand versions, like += and -=, for concise variable updates.

One important aspect of working with variables is understanding scope. Scope defines where in your code a variable is accessible and where it isn't. In JavaScript, there are two main types of scope: "global" and "local" (or "function") scope. Variables declared outside of any function are considered global and can be accessed from anywhere in your code. On the other hand, variables declared inside a function are local to that function and can only be accessed within the function.

Block scope is a newer concept in JavaScript, introduced with the let and const keywords. Variables declared with let and const in block scope are only accessible within the block in which they are declared. This allows for more fine-grained control over variable visibility and prevents unintended variable leakage.

One common challenge in JavaScript programming is type coercion. Type coercion occurs when the language automatically converts a value from one data type to another. For example, when you concatenate a number and a string, JavaScript coerces the number to a string and performs the concatenation. While type coercion can be convenient, it can also lead to unexpected behavior. To avoid surprises, it's essential to be aware of how type coercion works and explicitly convert values when necessary.

The typeof operator is a valuable tool for checking the data type of a value. It returns a string indicating the data type of the operand. You can use it to conditionally execute code based on the data type of a variable. For example, you might use typeof to check if a variable is a number before performing arithmetic operations on it.

JavaScript provides a variety of built-in functions and methods for working with data. For instance, you can use the parseInt() function to convert a string to an integer, or the parseFloat() function to convert a string to a floating-point number. The String object has methods like toUpperCase() and toLowerCase() for changing the case of characters in a string. Arrays, which are used to store collections of data, come with methods like push(), pop(), shift(), and unshift() for adding and removing elements. These built-in functions and methods can save you time and effort when working with data.

In JavaScript, you can also create custom functions to encapsulate reusable pieces of code. A function is a block of code that can be invoked and executed whenever needed. Functions can take parameters, which act as inputs, and can return values as outputs. To declare a function, you use the function keyword, followed by a function name, a parameter list enclosed in parentheses, and a block of code enclosed in curly braces. You can then call the function by its name and provide arguments as values for the parameters.

Scope also plays a significant role in functions. Variables declared inside a function are usually local to that function and cannot be accessed from outside. However, variables declared in a higher-level scope, such as in a parent function or in the global scope, can be accessed within nested functions. This concept is known as "lexical scoping" or "closure."

JavaScript also supports anonymous functions, which are functions without a named identifier. These functions can be assigned to variables or used as arguments to other functions. One common use of anonymous functions is in callbacks, where they are often passed as arguments to functions like addEventListener() for event handling.

Operators play a crucial role in performing operations within functions. You can use operators to manipulate data, make decisions, and control the flow of your code. For example, you might use the + operator to concatenate strings within a function, or the if statement to create conditional logic.

Understanding the concept of "truthy" and "falsy" values is essential when working with conditions in JavaScript. In JavaScript, values are not strictly true or false; they are evaluated as truthy or falsy based on their inherent "truthiness." Falsy values include false, 0, '' (empty string), null, undefined, and NaN, while all other values are considered truthy. Knowing which values are falsy helps you write more concise and readable conditional statements.

One powerful feature of JavaScript is the ability to create complex data structures using objects and arrays. Objects are used to store collections of key-value pairs, while arrays are used to store ordered collections of values. Both objects and arrays can be nested, allowing you to create hierarchical data structures.

Accessing and manipulating data within objects and arrays often involves using dot notation or square brackets. For example, you can access an object's property using object.property or an array element using array[index]. You can also use methods like push(), pop(), and splice() to add or remove elements from arrays. When dealing with objects, you can add, update, or delete properties using dot notation or square brackets.

In JavaScript, operators can also be applied to objects and arrays. For instance, the + operator can concatenate arrays or concatenate strings within an array. You can use operators like == and === to compare objects and arrays, but keep in mind that they compare references rather than content. To compare the content of arrays or objects, you need to iterate through their elements or properties manually.

In summary, variables, data types, and operators form the foundation of JavaScript programming. They enable you to store, manipulate, and control data in your code. Understanding how to declare variables, work with different data types, and use operators is essential for writing effective JavaScript programs. As you progress in your JavaScript journey, you'll find these concepts to be the building blocks upon which you can create more complex and sophisticated applications.

Control structures and functions are two fundamental building blocks of any programming language, including JavaScript. Next, we'll delve deeper into these concepts, exploring how they shape the flow and logic of your code. Control structures, such as conditional statements and loops, provide the means to make decisions and repeat tasks. Conditional statements, like if, else if, and else, allow your code to make choices based on conditions. These conditions can evaluate to either true or false, and they determine which code block is executed. Conditional statements are essential for adding logic and interactivity to your programs.

The if statement is the simplest form of a conditional statement. It evaluates a condition and executes a block of code if the condition is true. You can also extend the if statement with else if and else clauses to handle multiple conditions. This allows you to create branching logic, where different code blocks are executed based on different conditions. For example, you can use else if clauses to provide alternative paths of execution when the initial condition is false, and the else clause to handle the default case when none of the previous conditions are met.

Switch statements are another way to handle multiple conditions in JavaScript. A switch statement evaluates an expression and compares it to a series of case values. When a match is found, the corresponding code block is executed. Switch statements can be more concise than a series of if and else if statements, especially when you have many conditions to check. However, they can only compare the expression to exact values, and they don't support complex conditions.

Loops are essential for performing repetitive tasks in your code. JavaScript offers several types of loops, each suited for different scenarios. The for loop is used when you know the number of iterations in advance. It consists of three parts: initialization, condition, and increment (or decrement) statement. The loop iterates as long as the condition evaluates to true, executing the specified code block in each iteration. The for loop is commonly used for iterating over arrays and performing a specific action for each item.

The while loop, on the other hand, continues executing as long as a specified condition remains true. It doesn't require an initial iteration count like the for loop. The while loop is suitable when you don't know the exact number of iterations in advance, and you want to keep iterating until a certain condition is met. It's essential to ensure that the condition eventually becomes false to prevent an infinite loop.

The do...while loop is similar to the while loop, but it guarantees that the code block is executed at least once. In a do...while loop, the code block is executed first, and then the condition is checked. If the condition is true, the loop continues, and if it's false, the loop terminates. This type of loop is useful when you want to ensure that a specific task is performed before evaluating the condition.

For more complex looping scenarios, JavaScript provides the for...in and for...of loops. The for...in loop is designed for iterating over the properties of an object. It's especially handy when you need to enumerate the keys of an object or iterate through the properties of an array-like object. On the other hand, the for...of loop is used to iterate over the values of iterable objects, such as arrays, strings, and collections. It provides a concise way to access and process the elements of an iterable.

Functions are an integral part of structuring your code and making it more organized and reusable. A function is a block of code that performs a specific task or calculates a value. Functions help you break down your code into manageable, self-contained units, making it easier to debug, maintain, and collaborate on projects.

In JavaScript, you can declare functions using the function keyword, followed by a name, a parameter list, and a block of code enclosed in curly braces. For example, here's a simple function that adds two numbers:

javascriptCopy code

```
function addNumbers(a, b) { return a + b; }
```

Functions can take parameters as inputs, perform operations, and return results. In the example above, addNumbers takes two parameters, a and b, and returns their sum. You can call this function by providing arguments for a and b, like this:

javascriptCopy code

```
const result = addNumbers(5, 3);
```

Functions can also be defined as anonymous functions, which do not have a name. Anonymous functions are often used as arguments to other functions or as callbacks. For example:

javascriptCopy code

```
const double = function(x) { return x * 2; };
```

In modern JavaScript, you can use arrow functions as a concise way to define functions. Arrow functions have a shorter syntax and automatically bind the this value. Here's the previous double function redefined as an arrow function:

javascriptCopy code

```
const double = x => x * 2;
```

One crucial concept in JavaScript is "scope," which determines the visibility and accessibility of variables within your code. JavaScript has function scope, which means that variables declared within a function are only accessible within that function. However, variables declared outside of any function have "global scope" and can be accessed from anywhere in your code. Understanding scope is essential for avoiding variable naming conflicts and managing the lifetime of variables.

Closures are an advanced concept related to scope in JavaScript. A closure is a function that "remembers" the environment in which it was created, including the variables and values from its parent function's scope. This allows closures to access and manipulate variables even after the parent function has finished executing. Closures are often used to create private variables and encapsulate functionality within a function.

JavaScript also supports the concept of "hoisting," which means that variable and function declarations are moved to the top of their containing scope during the compilation phase. While variable declarations using var are hoisted, their initializations are not. This can lead to unexpected behavior if you're not aware of hoisting. To avoid hoisting-related issues, it's recommended to declare and initialize variables at the top of their respective scopes.

Another essential aspect of functions in JavaScript is their ability to return values. Functions can return values using the return statement, which specifies the value to be returned. The calling code can then capture and use the returned value. Functions can have multiple return statements, but once a return statement is executed, the function exits, and no further code is executed.

Function parameters can have default values in JavaScript, which is useful when you want to provide a fallback value if an argument is not passed when the function is called. Default parameter values are specified in the function's parameter list and are used when the corresponding argument is undefined.

JavaScript also supports "rest parameters" and "spread operators" for working with variable numbers of function arguments. Rest parameters allow you to capture multiple function arguments into an array, making it easier to work with dynamic inputs. Spread operators, on the other hand, allow you to spread the elements of an array or object into separate arguments or properties.

Recursion is another powerful technique in JavaScript, where a function calls itself to solve a problem or perform a task. Recursive functions are often used to solve problems that can be broken down into smaller, similar subproblems. A classic example of recursion is the calculation of factorial numbers.

In summary, control structures and functions are essential components of JavaScript programming. Control structures, including conditional statements and loops, help you create decision-making and repetitive logic in your code. Functions allow you to encapsulate code into reusable units, improving code organization and maintainability. Understanding scope, closures, hoisting, and function parameters is crucial for writing effective JavaScript code. By mastering these concepts, you'll be well-equipped to create sophisticated and robust JavaScript applications.

Chapter 2: ES6 Essentials: Arrow Functions, Classes, and Modules

Arrow functions, introduced in ECMAScript 6 (ES6), have become a popular feature in modern JavaScript development due to their concise syntax and the way they handle the this keyword. Arrow functions are a shorthand way to define functions in JavaScript, offering some key benefits over traditional function expressions. One of the most significant advantages of arrow functions is their shorter syntax, which can make your code cleaner and more readable. Instead of using the function keyword, arrow functions use a concise => syntax.

Here's a basic example of an arrow function that calculates the square of a number:

javascriptCopy code

```
const square = ( x ) => x * x;
```

In this example, the arrow function takes a single parameter x and returns the result of x multiplied by itself. The parentheses around the parameter x are optional when there's only one parameter, making the syntax even more concise.

Arrow functions are particularly useful when you need to write short, simple functions. For functions that consist of a single expression, you can omit the curly braces {} and the return keyword. The result of the expression is automatically returned.

For instance, you can use an arrow function to create a function that adds two numbers:

javascriptCopy code

```javascript
const add = (a, b) => a + b;
```

In this case, the arrow function takes two parameters, a and b, and returns their sum. The concise syntax of arrow functions is especially beneficial for defining callback functions, which are commonly used in JavaScript for asynchronous operations and event handling.

Arrow functions also have lexical scoping for the this keyword, which means they inherit the value of this from their surrounding code. In contrast, traditional function expressions have their own this value, which can lead to unexpected behavior and confusion.

Consider the following example, where we have an object with a method that defines a traditional function as a callback:

javascriptCopy code

```javascript
const person = { name: 'John', sayHello: function() {
console.log(`Hello, my name is ${this.name}`); } };
```

In this case, this inside the sayHello method refers to the person object, and it correctly logs the person's name.

However, if we define the callback function using an arrow function, like this:

javascriptCopy code

```javascript
const person = { name: 'John', sayHello: () => {
console.log(`Hello, my name is ${this.name}`); } };
```

The this keyword inside the arrow function will not refer to the person object but will instead inherit the value of this from the surrounding scope. This can lead to unexpected results, as this.name will likely be undefined.

Arrow functions are especially beneficial when working with functions inside functions, such as callbacks within callbacks. In these situations, the lexical scoping of arrow functions can help you avoid the need to bind this manually or use workarounds like storing this in a separate variable.

Another advantage of arrow functions is that they cannot be used as constructors to create new objects. In other words, you cannot use the new keyword with an arrow function to create instances of objects. This limitation can be advantageous in preventing unintended errors, as arrow functions are designed to be used for concise, stateless functions rather than constructor functions.

It's worth noting that arrow functions are not suitable for all scenarios. Their simplicity and concise syntax make them ideal for short, straightforward functions, but they may not be the best choice for more complex functions that require multiple statements or have intricate logic. In such cases, traditional function expressions with curly braces and a return statement may be more appropriate.

Additionally, arrow functions do not have their own arguments object. The arguments object is an array-like object available in traditional functions that contains all the arguments passed to the function. Arrow functions rely on the arguments of their containing function, which can lead to unexpected behavior if you're not aware of this difference.

For example, in a traditional function expression, you can access the arguments object to work with all the passed arguments, even if the function doesn't explicitly declare parameters:

javascriptCopy code

```
function sum() { let total = 0; for (let i = 0; i < arguments.length; i++) { total += arguments[i]; } return total; }
```

In this function, the arguments object allows you to handle any number of arguments passed to the sum function.

However, if you try to use the arguments object inside an arrow function, it will refer to the arguments of the containing function, not the arrow function itself. This can lead to unexpected behavior, as demonstrated in the following code:

javascriptCopy code

```
function add() { const arrowFunction = () => { console.log(arguments.length); // Outputs the number of arguments in the containing function, not the arrow function }; arrowFunction(); } add(1, 2, 3);
```

In this example, the arguments object inside the arrow function refers to the arguments of the add function, not the arrowFunction.

To summarize, arrow functions are a valuable addition to JavaScript, offering concise syntax and lexical scoping for the this keyword. They are especially well-suited for short, simple functions and callback functions. However, they may not be suitable for all scenarios, particularly when dealing with complex logic or functions that require access to their own arguments object. Understanding the strengths and limitations of arrow functions will help you use them effectively in your JavaScript code.

In modern JavaScript development, ES6 (ECMAScript 2015) introduced several features that enhance the language's capabilities, including classes and modules. These features have significantly improved code organization, reusability, and maintainability. ES6 classes provide a more structured and familiar way to define and work with objects and constructors. Before ES6, JavaScript primarily used constructor functions and prototypes to create objects and define their behavior. While this approach worked, it had limitations and could become complex for larger projects.

ES6 classes simplify the process of creating objects and defining their methods and properties. A class is like a blueprint for creating objects, and it encapsulates both data and functionality. To declare a class in JavaScript, you use the class keyword followed by the class name. Here's a simple example of defining a class called Person:

javascriptCopy code

```
class Person { constructor(name, age) { this.name = name; this.age = age; } greet() { return `Hello, my name is ${this.name} and I am ${this.age} years old.`; } }
```

In this example, the Person class has a constructor method that initializes the name and age properties when a new Person object is created. The greet method is defined within the class and allows instances of Person to display a greeting message.

To create an instance of a class, you use the new keyword followed by the class name and any necessary constructor arguments. For example:

javascriptCopy code

```
const john = new Person('John', 30);
```

Now, john is an instance of the Person class with the name property set to 'John' and the age property set to 30. You can call the greet method on john to get a greeting message.

ES6 classes also support inheritance, allowing you to create subclasses that inherit properties and methods from a parent class. To create a subclass, you use the extends keyword, and you can override or extend the behavior of the parent class. Here's an example of creating a Student class that extends the Person class:

javascriptCopy code

```
class Student extends Person { constructor(name, age, grade) { super(name, age); // Call the constructor of the parent class this.grade = grade; } study() { return `${this.name} is studying hard to achieve a grade of ${this.grade}.`; } }
```

In this example, the Student class inherits the name and age properties from the Person class using the super keyword to call the parent class's constructor. It also defines a study method specific to students.

You can create instances of the Student class just like you would with the Person class, and they will inherit the greet method from the parent class and have access to their own study method.

javascriptCopy code

```
const jane = new Student('Jane', 25, 'A');
```

The import and export statements introduced in ES6 enable modular code organization and help manage dependencies between different parts of your JavaScript application. Before ES6, developers relied on global variables and complex scripts to achieve similar functionality. With modules, you can encapsulate code into separate files and selectively export and import functions, classes, or variables to control what is accessible from other modules.

To create a module in JavaScript, you define your code in a separate file and use the export keyword to specify what should be accessible from outside the module. For example, you can create a module called math.js with the following content:

javascriptCopy code

```
// math.js export function add(a, b) { return a + b; }
export function subtract(a, b) { return a - b; }
```

In this module, the add and subtract functions are explicitly exported using the export keyword. These functions can be imported and used in other modules.

To import functions or variables from a module, you use the import statement in your JavaScript code. For instance, if you want to use the add function from the math.js module, you can import it like this:

javascriptCopy code

```
import { add } from './math.js'; const result = add(5,
3); // result is 8
```

The import statement specifies what you want to import from the module, and you must provide the relative path to the module file. This allows you to use the exported functions or variables as if they were defined in your current module.

ES6 modules support both named exports, as shown in the previous example, and default exports. A default export is used when you want to export a single "main" value from a module. To export a default value, you use the export default syntax.

Here's an example of exporting and importing a default value:

javascriptCopy code

```javascript
// math.js export default function add(a, b) { return a + b; }
```

javascriptCopy code

```javascript
// main.js import add from './math.js'; const result = add(5, 3); // result is 8
```

In this case, the add function is the default export of the math.js module, and you can import it without curly braces.

ES6 classes and modules have greatly improved the structure and organization of JavaScript code. Classes provide a more intuitive way to create and manage objects, while modules enable you to organize your code into reusable and encapsulated units. These features have become essential tools in modern JavaScript development, making it easier to build and maintain complex applications while improving code readability and reusability. Understanding how to leverage ES6 classes and modules is crucial for any JavaScript developer looking to write clean and maintainable code.

In modern JavaScript development, asynchronous operations are a common part of web applications, and they often involve tasks like fetching data from a server, reading files, or waiting for user interactions. Asynchronous code is essential to keep applications responsive and efficient, but it can quickly become complex and hard to manage using traditional callback-based methods. To address this challenge, ECMAScript 2017 (ES8) introduced async and await, which offer a more concise and readable way to work with asynchronous code.

The async and await keywords provide a cleaner and more straightforward syntax for handling asynchronous operations in JavaScript. Before their introduction, developers primarily used callbacks and promises to manage asynchronous tasks. While these methods were functional, they could lead to deeply nested code structures known as "callback hell" or "pyramid of doom," making the code difficult to understand and maintain.

With async and await, you can write asynchronous code that resembles synchronous code in terms of readability and structure. An async function is a function that always returns a promise, allowing you to use the await keyword within the function to pause execution until a promise is resolved or rejected.

Here's an example of an async function that uses the await keyword to pause execution until a promise is resolved:

javascriptCopy code

```
async function fetchData() { const response = await fetch('https://api.example.com/data'); const data = await response.json(); return data; }
```

In this code, the fetchData function fetches data from an API using the fetch function and then parses the JSON response using response.json(). The await keyword is used before both fetch and response.json() to wait for the promises to be resolved before continuing.

Using async and await not only makes asynchronous code cleaner but also allows for better error handling. You can use a try...catch block to handle any errors that occur during the asynchronous operation:

```javascript
javascriptCopy code
async function fetchData() { try { const response = await fetch('https://api.example.com/data'); if (!response.ok) { throw new Error('Failed to fetch data'); } const data = await response.json(); return data; } catch (error) { console.error('An error occurred:', error); throw error; // Rethrow the error to propagate it } }
```

In this example, if the fetch request fails or if there is an issue parsing the JSON response, the code inside the catch block will execute, allowing you to handle errors gracefully.

async and await also make it easier to handle multiple asynchronous tasks in a more readable and sequential manner. In the following example, an async function fetches data from two different endpoints sequentially:

```javascript
javascriptCopy code
async function fetchData() { const data1 = await fetch('https://api.example.com/data1').then(response => response.json()); const data2 = await fetch('https://api.example.com/data2').then(response => response.json()); return { data1, data2 }; }
```

Here, the await keyword is used to pause the function execution until each fetch request is complete. This approach allows you to handle each request one at a time, making the code more intuitive.

In addition to making asynchronous code more readable, async and await also improve error handling. In a traditional callback-based approach or when working with promises directly, you might need to handle errors in each step of the asynchronous process. With async and await, you can use a single try...catch block to catch and handle errors for the entire asynchronous operation, simplifying error handling logic.

However, it's important to note that async and await are not a replacement for promises but rather a more ergonomic way to work with them. Behind the scenes, async functions still return promises, and await is used to wait for promises to resolve. This means that you can mix async and await with existing promise-based code seamlessly.

Here's an example of mixing async and await with promises:

javascriptCopy code

```
async function fetchData() { const response = await fetch('https://api.example.com/data'); const data = await response.json(); return data; } fetchData()
.then(data => { console.log('Data fetched:', data); })
.catch(error => { console.error('An error occurred:', error); });
```

In this code, the fetchData function is defined as an async function and returns a promise. You can use the .then and .catch methods to handle the result or error of the promise returned by fetchData.

While async and await offer many benefits for handling asynchronous code, it's important to be aware of their limitations. For example, they cannot be used in top-level code outside of functions or modules. You can only use await within an async function.

Another consideration is that await makes code execution pause until the awaited promise is resolved. While this can be beneficial for sequential operations, it may not be suitable for scenarios where you want to execute multiple tasks concurrently. In such cases, you can use features like Promise.all to parallelize asynchronous tasks.

In summary, async and await are powerful additions to JavaScript that simplify the management of asynchronous code. They provide a cleaner and more readable syntax for handling asynchronous operations, making it easier to write and maintain code that deals with tasks like network requests, file I/O, and more. Understanding how to use async and await effectively is a valuable skill for modern JavaScript developers looking to improve the clarity and maintainability of their code.

Chapter 4: Advanced DOM Manipulation and Event Delegation

As web developers, manipulating the Document Object Model (DOM) is a fundamental skill that allows us to create dynamic and interactive web applications. The DOM represents the structure of an HTML document, including all the elements and their relationships, and provides a way to access and modify this structure using JavaScript. While basic DOM manipulation is a common practice, advanced techniques can take your web development skills to the next level.

One of the first advanced techniques to explore is event delegation, which is a powerful method for handling events efficiently. Instead of attaching event listeners to individual elements, event delegation involves attaching a single event listener to a common ancestor of those elements. When an event occurs, it bubbles up through the DOM hierarchy, and the ancestor can catch and handle the event on behalf of its descendants. This approach is particularly useful when dealing with a large number of elements, such as a list of items.

Event delegation can help improve performance and reduce memory consumption since you only need one event listener, even if you have many elements. It also simplifies the process of adding or removing elements dynamically, as you don't need to attach or detach event listeners individually for each element.

Here's an example of event delegation:

javascriptCopy code

```
document.getElementById('list-container').addEventListener('click', function(event) {
if (event.target.tagName === 'LI') { // Handle the click on an individual list item
event.target.classList.toggle('selected'); } });
```

In this code, the event listener is attached to the list-container element, and it checks if the clicked element is an LI element. If it is, the code toggles the selected class for that list item. This way, you can handle clicks on any list item without attaching individual listeners to each one.

Another advanced DOM manipulation technique involves working with the textContent and innerHTML properties. While these properties are commonly used for getting and setting text content and HTML content, respectively, they can also be leveraged creatively to manipulate the DOM.

For example, you can use textContent to replace the content of an element, effectively removing all its child elements and text while preserving the element itself:

javascriptCopy code

```
const element = document.getElementById('my-element'); element.textContent = 'New content';
```

Similarly, you can use innerHTML to insert or replace HTML content within an element:

javascriptCopy code

```javascript
const element = document.getElementById('my-element'); element.innerHTML = '<p>This is <em>new</em> content.</p>';
```

However, it's important to exercise caution when using innerHTML to prevent security risks, such as cross-site scripting (XSS) attacks. Always sanitize and validate any user-generated content before injecting it into your page's HTML.

In addition to event delegation and manipulating content, understanding the classList property can greatly enhance your DOM manipulation skills. The classList property allows you to work with an element's classes, including adding, removing, toggling, and checking for the presence of classes.

For example, you can add a class to an element like this:

javascriptCopy code

```javascript
const element = document.getElementById('my-element'); element.classList.add('highlight');
```

You can also remove a class:

javascriptCopy code

```javascript
element.classList.remove('highlight');
```

Or toggle a class on and off:

javascriptCopy code

```javascript
element.classList.toggle('highlight');
```

Using classList simplifies the process of applying styles and behavior to elements in response to user interactions or other events. It's a cleaner and more maintainable way to manage class-related changes compared to manually manipulating the className property.

Another advanced technique is working with custom data attributes, which allow you to store additional data directly in your HTML elements. Custom data attributes are prefixed with data- and can hold any value you need. These attributes are accessible via the dataset property in JavaScript.

Here's an example of using custom data attributes:

htmlCopy code

```html
<div id="product" data-product-id="12345" data-price="29.99" data-in-stock="true"></div>
```

In JavaScript, you can access these data attributes like this:

javascriptCopy code

```javascript
const product = document.getElementById('product');
const productId = product.dataset.productId; // "12345"
const price = parseFloat(product.dataset.price); // 29.99
const inStock = product.dataset.inStock === 'true'; // true
```

Custom data attributes provide a convenient way to associate metadata with elements, making it easier to work with data-driven applications.

As you delve deeper into advanced DOM manipulation, you may encounter situations where you need to clone and manipulate elements. The cloneNode method allows you to create a deep copy of an element, including all its child nodes. You can then insert the cloned element elsewhere in the DOM, modify it as needed, or use it as a template.

Here's an example of cloning an element:

javascriptCopy code

```
const          originalElement          =
document.getElementById('original');          const
clonedElement = originalElement.cloneNode(true); //
true indicates a deep clone clonedElement.id =
'cloned';
document.body.appendChild(clonedElement);
```

In this code, the cloneNode method creates a deep copy of the originalElement along with all its child nodes. You can then modify the clonedElement or insert it into the DOM as required.

Advanced DOM manipulation techniques also include working with animation and transitions. You can use CSS transitions and animations to create smooth and visually appealing effects on your web pages. By applying CSS classes dynamically or using JavaScript to modify CSS properties, you can trigger animations and transitions based on user interactions or other events.

Additionally, libraries like GreenSock Animation Platform (GSAP) provide powerful tools for creating complex animations with JavaScript. These libraries offer more control and flexibility than CSS alone, allowing you to build interactive and visually stunning web applications.

Finally, when working with complex web applications, you may need to manage the state of your application and efficiently update the DOM in response to changes. Libraries like React, Angular, and Vue.js provide advanced state management and component-based architectures, making it easier to build and maintain large-scale applications.

In summary, advanced DOM manipulation techniques are crucial for building interactive and dynamic web applications. Event delegation, manipulating content, working with class lists, custom data attributes, cloning elements, and handling animations and transitions are all essential skills for web developers. By mastering these techniques, you can create more efficient, maintainable, and visually engaging web applications that delight your users and provide a seamless user experience.

In the world of web development, event handling is a fundamental concept. It allows you to create interactive and responsive web applications by responding to user actions such as clicks, keypresses, and mouse movements. While handling events on individual elements is straightforward, it can become unwieldy when dealing with a large number of elements or dynamically generated content. This is where event delegation comes into play—a powerful technique that simplifies event handling and improves performance.

Event delegation is an approach where you attach a single event listener to a common ancestor element (usually higher up the DOM tree) instead of attaching multiple listeners to individual child elements. When an event occurs on a child element, it bubbles up to the ancestor element, where the event listener can respond accordingly. This strategy reduces the number of event listeners in your code and simplifies the maintenance of event handling logic.

Imagine you have a list of items, each represented by an <li> element, and you want to do something when any of them is clicked. A common approach would be to attach a click event listener to each <li> element individually:

javascriptCopy code

```
const    items    =    document.querySelectorAll('li');
items.forEach(item => { item.addEventListener('click',
() => { // Handle the click on each item }); });
```

While this works, it can be inefficient and lead to performance issues, especially if the list contains a large number of items. With event delegation, you can handle all clicks on a common ancestor element, such as a <ul> containing the list items:

javascriptCopy code

```
const    list    =    document.querySelector('ul');
list.addEventListener('click',    event    =>    {    const
clickedItem = event.target; if (clickedItem.tagName
=== 'LI') { // Handle the click on any list item } });
```

In this example, a single event listener is attached to the <ul> element. When a click event occurs on any <li> element within the list, it bubbles up to the <ul>, where the event listener checks if the clicked element is an <li> before proceeding. This approach is more efficient and scalable, as you only need one event listener regardless of the number of list items.

Event delegation is particularly useful for scenarios where elements are added or removed dynamically from the DOM. Since the event listener is attached to a static ancestor element, it automatically applies to any new elements that match the criteria (e.g., <li> elements) added later, without requiring additional event binding.

Another advantage of event delegation is that it simplifies the code, making it easier to understand and maintain. You don't need to worry about attaching and removing event listeners dynamically as elements are created or destroyed. The event handler logic remains centralized, which can enhance code organization and reduce potential bugs.

However, when implementing event delegation, it's essential to be mindful of a few considerations. Firstly, you should always check the target element (accessed via event.target) to ensure it matches the expected criteria. In the example above, we verified that the clicked element is an <li> before proceeding. This step helps prevent unintended behavior when clicks occur on other elements within the <ul>.

Secondly, keep in mind that events bubble up the DOM tree. If you have nested elements with event delegation, the event will propagate up through all the ancestors. Consider this example with nested lists:

htmlCopy code

```
<ul id="parent"> <li>Item 1</li> <li> Item 2 <ul id="child"> <li>Subitem 1</li> <li>Subitem 2</li> </ul> </li> </ul>
```

If you attach an event listener to the <ul> element with the id "parent" and click on a subitem, the event will bubble up to the parent <ul>, potentially triggering the event handler unintentionally. You can mitigate this by checking the target element and ensuring it matches your expected criteria.

Additionally, be aware that some events, such as focus and blur, do not bubble by default. For these events, you might need to use a capturing phase event listener or attach the listener directly to the target elements.

In summary, event delegation is a valuable technique for efficient event handling in web development. By attaching a single event listener to a common ancestor element, you can simplify your code, improve performance, and handle dynamically generated content gracefully. When implementing event delegation, always verify the target element, consider event propagation in nested structures, and adapt for non-bubbling events when necessary. Mastering event delegation is a skill that will make your web applications more responsive and maintainable.

State management is a crucial aspect of building web applications, as it involves storing, managing, and updating data that influences the behavior and appearance of your application. Web applications often require various types of state, such as user input, UI state, and data fetched from servers. Managing this state effectively is essential for creating responsive and reliable applications. There are several state management techniques and libraries available for web development, each suited to different scenarios and requirements.

One of the simplest forms of state management is local state, where data is stored and managed within individual components or modules. This approach is suitable for handling state that is specific to a single component and does not need to be shared with other parts of the application. Local state is typically managed using the component's internal state variables or hooks, such as useState in React. For example, you might use local state to control the visibility of a modal dialog within a specific component.

javascriptCopy code

```
import React, { useState } from 'react'; function Modal() { const [isOpen, setIsOpen] = useState(false); const openModal = () => { setIsOpen(true); }; const closeModal = () => { setIsOpen(false); }; return ( <div> <button onClick={openModal}>Open Modal</button> {isOpen && ( <div className="modal"> {/* Modal content */} <button onClick={closeModal}>Close Modal</button> </div> )} </div> ); }
```

While local state is straightforward and suitable for managing isolated state, it becomes less practical when you need to share and synchronize state across multiple components. For scenarios like these, you may consider using a state management library or pattern like prop drilling.

Prop drilling involves passing state down through the component hierarchy by passing props from parent components to child components. This approach can work well for small to medium-sized applications but can lead to issues in larger applications with deep component trees. As you pass state through intermediate components, it can become challenging to maintain and debug.

javascriptCopy code

```
function ParentComponent() { const [count, setCount] = useState(0); return ( <div> <h1>Count: {count}</h1> <ChildComponent count={count} setCount={setCount} /> </div> ); } function ChildComponent({ count,
```

```
setCount }) { const increment = () => { setCount(count
+ 1); }; return ( <div> <button
onClick={increment}>Increment</button> </div> ); }
```

In the above example, the count state and its updater function are passed down through the ParentComponent to the ChildComponent. While this works for a small example, in a larger application, you might encounter challenges tracking state changes and maintaining the flow of props.

To address these challenges, you can explore state management solutions that provide a centralized store for your application's data. Redux, for instance, is a popular state management library for React applications. It provides a global store where you can centralize and manage your application's state, making it accessible to any component in the application.

With Redux, you define actions to describe state changes and reducers to specify how those actions should modify the state. Components can connect to the Redux store to access and update the state as needed.

javascriptCopy code

```
// Redux actions const incrementAction = { type:
'INCREMENT' }; const decrementAction = { type:
'DECREMENT' }; // Redux reducer function
counterReducer(state = 0, action) { switch
(action.type) { case 'INCREMENT': return state + 1;
case 'DECREMENT': return state - 1; default: return
state; } } // Redux store const { createStore } = Redux;
```

```
const store = createStore(counterReducer); // React
component connected to Redux function Counter() {
const count = store.getState(); const increment = () =>
{ store.dispatch(incrementAction); }; const decrement
= () => { store.dispatch(decrementAction); }; return (
<div>      <h1>Count:      {count}</h1>      <button
onClick={increment}>Increment</button>      <button
onClick={decrement}>Decrement</button> </div> ); }
```

Redux provides a structured way to manage state in your application, making it easier to track and debug state changes. However, it also introduces additional complexity with actions, reducers, and store setup, which may be overkill for smaller projects.

Another state management solution for React applications is the Context API, introduced as part of React's core library. Context allows you to create a global state that can be accessed by any component within the component tree without the need for prop drilling.

```
javascriptCopy code
import React, { createContext, useContext, useReducer
} from 'react'; // Create a context const
CounterContext = createContext(); // Initial state and
reducer const initialState = { count: 0 }; function
counterReducer(state, action) { switch (action.type) {
case 'INCREMENT': return { count: state.count + 1 };
case 'DECREMENT': return { count: state.count - 1 };
default: return state; } } // Counter provider
component function CounterProvider({ children }) {
```

```
const [state, dispatch] = useReducer(counterReducer,
initialState); return ( <CounterContext.Provider
value={{ state, dispatch }}> {children}
</CounterContext.Provider> ); } // Custom hook to
access context function useCounter() { const context
= useContext(CounterContext); if (!context) { throw
new Error('useCounter must be used within a
CounterProvider'); } return context; } // React
component connected to context function Counter() {
const { state, dispatch } = useCounter(); const
increment = () => { dispatch({ type: 'INCREMENT' }); };
const decrement = () => { dispatch({ type:
'DECREMENT' }); }; return ( <div> <h1>Count:
{state.count}</h1> <button
onClick={increment}>Increment</button> <button
onClick={decrement}>Decrement</button> </div> ); }
```

The Context API simplifies state management in React by providing a centralized state accessible throughout the component tree. However, it may not offer the same level of features and tooling as dedicated state management libraries like Redux.

In addition to Redux and the Context API, there are other state management libraries and patterns available for various JavaScript frameworks, such as Mobx for React or Vuex for Vue.js. These libraries offer different approaches to state management, and the choice often depends on the specific needs and complexity of your application.

In summary, state management is a crucial aspect of web application development. Local state, prop drilling, libraries like Redux, and the Context API are all valuable tools for managing state in your applications. Choosing the right approach depends on factors like the size and complexity of your project, your familiarity with the tools, and your team's preferences. By mastering state management, you can create web applications that are responsive, maintainable, and capable of handling complex data flows.

In the ever-evolving landscape of web development, making asynchronous requests is a fundamental skill that enables web applications to interact with remote servers and fetch or send data without requiring a page reload. This capability, often achieved using AJAX (Asynchronous JavaScript and XML), has become a cornerstone of modern web development. AJAX allows you to create dynamic and interactive web applications that provide a seamless user experience. At its core, AJAX is a technique that allows you to send HTTP requests and retrieve data from a server in the background, without disrupting the user's current interaction with a web page. This asynchronous behavior is essential for tasks like fetching data from a server, submitting form data, or updating content dynamically without reloading the entire page. AJAX requests can work with various data formats, including JSON, XML, HTML, and plain text, making them versatile for different use cases. To make an AJAX request, you typically use the XMLHttpRequest object or the newer fetch API, both of which are built into modern web browsers. The XMLHttpRequest approach has been around for a long time and is well-supported across browsers, making it a reliable choice. However, the fetch API offers a more modern and flexible way to perform asynchronous requests.

Here's an example of making an AJAX request using the fetch API to retrieve data from a remote server:
javascriptCopy code

```
fetch('https://api.example.com/data') .then(response
=> { if (!response.ok) { throw new Error('Network
response was not ok'); } return response.json(); })
.then(data => { // Use the retrieved data
console.log(data); }) .catch(error => { // Handle any
errors that occurred during the fetch
console.error('Fetch error:', error); });
```

In this example, fetch is used to send a GET request to the URL 'https://api.example.com/data'. Once the request is complete, the response is processed using the .then() method. If the response status is not within the range 200-299 (indicating a successful request), an error is thrown. Otherwise, the response is parsed as JSON, and the retrieved data is available for further processing. Another common use case for AJAX is sending data to the server, often in the form of POST or PUT requests. You can include data in the request body, such as form data or JSON payloads, to update or create resources on the server.

Here's an example of making a POST request with fetch to send data to a server:
javascriptCopy code

```
const postData = { username: 'john_doe', email:
'john@example.com',                                  };
fetch('https://api.example.com/users', { method:
'POST', headers: { 'Content-Type': 'application/json', },
```

```
body: JSON.stringify(postData), }) .then(response => {
if (!response.ok) { throw new Error('Network
response was not ok'); } return response.json(); })
.then(data => { // Handle the server's response
console.log(data); }) .catch(error => { // Handle any
errors that occurred during the request
console.error('Fetch error:', error); });
```

In this example, a POST request is made to
'https://api.example.com/users', and the postData
object is sent as a JSON payload in the request body.
The server processes the data and responds
accordingly. AJAX requests often involve handling
different HTTP status codes to determine whether the
request was successful or encountered an error.
Common status codes include 200 for a successful
request, 404 for a resource not found, and 500 for a
server error. By checking the response's status code and
handling errors accordingly, you can create robust and
reliable AJAX functionality in your applications. It's
important to note that modern web development has
introduced even more convenient methods for making
asynchronous requests. One such method is the
async/await syntax, which simplifies working with
promises and makes asynchronous code more readable.
With async/await, you can write asynchronous code
that resembles synchronous code, making it easier to
understand and maintain. Here's an example of making
an asynchronous GET request using async/await with
the fetch API:

javascriptCopy code

```
async function fetchData() { try { const response =
await       fetch('https://api.example.com/data');       if
(!response.ok) { throw new Error('Network response
was not ok'); } const data = await response.json(); //
Use the retrieved data console.log(data); } catch
(error) { // Handle any errors that occurred during the
fetch   console.error('Fetch   error:',   error);   }   }
fetchData();
```

In this async function, the await keyword is used to
pause execution until the asynchronous operation
(fetching data) is complete. This results in cleaner and
more sequential code compared to using .then() chains.

As web development evolves, so do the tools and
techniques for making asynchronous requests. While
AJAX is a fundamental concept, you have various
options for implementation, including the traditional
XMLHttpRequest, the newer fetch API, and the
async/await syntax. Choosing the right approach
depends on your project's requirements, your
familiarity with the tools, and your team's preferences.

In summary, AJAX is a foundational technique in web
development   that   enables   asynchronous
communication with servers, allowing web applications
to fetch and send data without page reloads. Whether
you choose the XMLHttpRequest, the fetch API, or
embrace async/await syntax, mastering asynchronous
requests is crucial for building responsive and
interactive web applications that provide a seamless
user experience.

In the realm of modern web development, data retrieval from remote sources is a common and critical task, and the Fetch API has emerged as a powerful tool for this purpose. The Fetch API is a native JavaScript interface that allows you to make network requests, typically to fetch data from web services and APIs. It provides a more user-friendly and versatile alternative to the older XMLHttpRequest (XHR) object, making it the preferred choice for many developers. The Fetch API is built on the Promise-based architecture, which simplifies the handling of asynchronous operations. Promises allow you to write more readable and structured code for managing asynchronous actions. When making a network request with the Fetch API, you receive a Promise that resolves with the response from the server.

Here's a basic example of using the Fetch API to retrieve data from a remote JSON API:

javascriptCopy code

```
fetch('https://jsonplaceholder.typicode.com/posts/1')
.then(response => { if (!response.ok) { throw new Error('Network response was not ok'); } return response.json(); }).then(data => { // Use the retrieved data console.log(data); }).catch(error => { // Handle any errors that occurred during the fetch console.error('Fetch error:', error); });
```

In this example, the fetch function is called with the URL of the remote resource. The response from the server is then processed using the .then() method, where you can check if the response status is within the success range (usually 200-299) and parse the response data as JSON. If any errors occur during the fetch, the .catch() block handles them gracefully.

The Fetch API provides various options for configuring requests, such as specifying HTTP methods, adding headers, and sending data in the request body. You can customize requests according to the requirements of the web service or API you are interacting with.

Here's an example of making a POST request with the Fetch API, including headers and a JSON payload:

javascriptCopy code

```
const postData = { title: 'Sample Post', body: 'This is a sample post.', userId: 1, };
fetch('https://jsonplaceholder.typicode.com/posts', {
method: 'POST', headers: { 'Content-Type':
'application/json', }, body: JSON.stringify(postData), })
.then(response => { if (!response.ok) { throw new
Error('Network response was not ok'); } return
response.json(); }) .then(data => { // Handle the
server's response console.log(data); }) .catch(error =>
{ // Handle any errors that occurred during the request
console.error('Fetch error:', error); });
```

In this POST request example, a JSON payload (postData) is included in the request body. Headers are also set to specify the content type as JSON. This demonstrates how you can tailor Fetch requests to meet the specific needs of your data retrieval or submission tasks.

One of the Fetch API's notable features is its support for handling different types of responses, such as JSON, text, HTML, or even binary data like images. You can use various methods like .json(), .text(), and .blob() to process the response data in the desired format.

Here's an example of fetching and displaying an image using the Fetch API:

```javascript
Copy code
fetch('https://example.com/image.jpg')
.then(response => { if (!response.ok) { throw new Error('Network response was not ok'); } return response.blob(); }) .then(imageBlob => { // Create an image element and set its source to the retrieved blob const img = document.createElement('img'); img.src = URL.createObjectURL(imageBlob); // Display the image on the web page document.body.appendChild(img); }) .catch(error => { // Handle any errors that occurred during the fetch console.error('Fetch error:', error); });
```

In this example, the .blob() method is used to retrieve the response as a binary blob, which is then used to create an image element. The image is displayed on the web page by appending it to the document body.

Another valuable aspect of the Fetch API is its support for handling CORS (Cross-Origin Resource Sharing) requests. Cross-origin requests are common when interacting with APIs hosted on different domains. The

Fetch API can handle CORS by default, and you can configure it further by setting CORS-related headers on the server or using CORS-related options in the request. While the Fetch API offers many advantages and is well-suited for modern web development, it's essential to consider browser compatibility. Most modern browsers support the Fetch API, but if you need to support older browsers, you might need to use a polyfill or consider alternatives like the XMLHttpRequest (XHR) object.

In summary, the Fetch API has become a cornerstone of modern web development for making asynchronous data retrieval requests. Its Promise-based architecture, versatility in handling different response types, and support for customizing requests make it a powerful tool. Whether you're fetching JSON data from a remote API, submitting form data, or retrieving binary assets like images, the Fetch API simplifies the process and enhances the user experience of your web applications.

In the realm of web development, the concept of client-side routing plays a pivotal role in the creation of single-page applications (SPAs). SPAs are web applications that load a single HTML page and dynamically update the content as the user interacts with the app, without the need for full-page refreshes. Client-side routing is the mechanism that enables navigation within SPAs by changing the URL and updating the displayed content accordingly.

Traditional multi-page web applications rely on server-side routing, where each page corresponds to a different URL path, and the server handles requests by serving complete HTML pages. In contrast, SPAs deliver a more seamless user experience by handling most of the routing and content updates on the client side. This approach significantly reduces the need for server requests and provides a faster and more responsive user interface.

Client-side routing is achieved by using JavaScript libraries or frameworks that intercept URL changes and render the appropriate content based on the requested route. One popular library for client-side routing is React Router, which is commonly used in React-based SPAs.

To illustrate client-side routing, let's consider a simple example of a SPA that has two pages: a home page and a contact page. In this scenario, we'll use React Router to handle routing within our application.

First, you would typically set up your project with React and React Router, either by using a build tool like Create React App or by configuring your build system manually. Once your project is set up, you can define your routes using React Router's <Route> component. In your application's main component, you would wrap your routes with a <BrowserRouter> or <HashRouter> to enable client-side routing.

Here's a basic example of defining routes in a React application:

javascriptCopy code

```
import React from 'react'; import { BrowserRouter as Router, Route, Switch } from 'react-router-dom'; import Home from './components/Home'; import Contact from './components/Contact'; function App() { return ( <Router> <Switch> <Route path="/" exact component={Home} /> <Route path="/contact" component={Contact} /> </Switch> </Router> ); } export default App;
```

In this example, we've imported the necessary components from React Router and defined two routes: one for the home page ("/") and another for the contact page ("/contact"). The exact prop on the home route ensures that it matches only when the URL is exactly "/".

Now, when a user navigates to your SPA, React Router will intercept the URL changes and render the appropriate component based on the route. If the user visits the home page, the Home component will be displayed; if they visit the contact page, the Contact component will be rendered.

Client-side routing also provides the ability to navigate programmatically within your SPA. You can use the Link component provided by React Router to create navigational links within your application.

Here's an example of using the Link component to create navigation links:

javascriptCopy code

```
import React from 'react'; import { Link } from 'react-router-dom'; function Navigation() { return ( <nav> <ul> <li> <Link to="/">Home</Link> </li> <li> <Link to="/contact">Contact</Link> </li> </ul> </nav> ); } export default Navigation;
```

In this Navigation component, we've used the Link component to create links to the home and contact pages. When a user clicks one of these links, React Router will update the URL and render the corresponding component.

One of the significant benefits of client-side routing is that it enables bookmarking and sharing of specific URLs. Since the URL changes when navigating within the SPA, users can bookmark or share a link to a particular page. When someone opens that link, the SPA will load the correct content based on the URL, providing a seamless experience.

Additionally, client-side routing allows for smooth transitions between pages without the need for full-page reloads. You can implement page transitions and animations to enhance the user experience further. While client-side routing offers numerous advantages, it also introduces some challenges. One challenge is handling routes that do not exist or handling 404 errors. In a traditional server-rendered application, the server would return a 404 page for non-existent routes. In a client-side routed SPA, you must implement your own error handling and route not found logic. Another challenge is managing the application's state and data fetching. In a multi-page application, you might fetch data when a user navigates to a specific page. In a SPA, you must decide whether to fetch data when the application initially loads or when a specific route is accessed. Managing the state and lifecycle of your components becomes crucial. In summary, client-side routing is a fundamental concept in building single-page applications (SPAs) that provide a seamless user experience. It enables navigation within the SPA by changing the URL and updating the displayed content without full-page reloads. Using libraries like React Router, you can define routes, create navigation links, and handle URL changes. Client-side routing enhances the speed and interactivity of web applications, making them more dynamic and user-friendly.

Chapter 9: Responsive Web Design and CSS Grid

In the world of web development, designing and building reusable UI components is a foundational practice that promotes efficiency, consistency, and maintainability in your projects. UI components are the building blocks of your user interfaces, representing specific pieces of functionality or visual elements. By creating these components to be reusable, you can save time and effort, ensure a cohesive design, and facilitate collaboration within your development team.

Reusability is a concept that extends beyond coding—it encompasses design, functionality, and user experience. When you design a UI component to be reusable, you're essentially creating a modular piece of your application that can be employed in different contexts without requiring significant modifications. This approach aligns with the principles of component-based architecture, where the user interface is constructed from reusable building blocks.

The first step in designing reusable UI components is identifying common patterns and elements within your application. For example, you might notice that several parts of your interface share similar styling or behavior, such as buttons, forms, or navigation menus. Recognizing these patterns allows you to abstract them into reusable components.

Once you've identified the components you want to create, you can design their interfaces or APIs. An API for a UI component defines how it can be used and configured by other parts of your application. Consider what customization options are necessary, such as props or configuration settings, to make the component adaptable to various requirements.

Let's take the example of a button component. A well-designed button component might allow you to customize its text, color, size, and behavior through props. This level of customization empowers developers to use the button in different contexts while maintaining a consistent design language.

When building reusable UI components, it's essential to separate concerns and adhere to the principle of single responsibility. Each component should have a specific purpose and should not encompass unrelated functionality. This separation of concerns not only makes components more maintainable but also encourages reusability.

Furthermore, consider the structure of your components. Divide your UI components into smaller, reusable sub-components if it makes sense. For instance, a complex form component might consist of smaller input field components, each responsible for its own validation and rendering.

Another important aspect of reusable UI components is theming and styling. Allowing developers to customize the appearance of components is crucial for integrating them into various designs. This can be achieved through CSS classes, CSS-in-JS solutions, or style props that accept inline styling.

Documentation is an often overlooked but critical component of building reusable UI components. Comprehensive documentation helps developers understand how to use the component, what props are available, and what the expected behavior is. Consider providing examples and use cases to showcase the component's versatility.

Testing is another crucial aspect of creating reusable UI components. Ensure that your components are thoroughly tested to catch any regressions or issues that may arise during development. Automated tests, such as unit tests and integration tests, can provide confidence in the reliability of your components.

Version control and package management also play a role in making UI components reusable. Consider packaging your components as standalone libraries or packages that can be easily shared and versioned using tools like npm or yarn. This approach allows you to manage dependencies and updates efficiently.

To encourage the adoption of reusable UI components within your development team, foster a culture of collaboration and knowledge sharing. Share your components in a central repository or package registry, and encourage other team members to contribute improvements and bug fixes. Creating a library of reusable components can significantly accelerate development and reduce duplicated efforts.

In addition to creating standalone components, consider incorporating a design system into your development process. A design system provides a comprehensive set of guidelines, patterns, and reusable components that ensure consistency in design and functionality across your application. It serves as a valuable resource for designers and developers, promoting a unified and polished user experience.

When it comes to designing and building reusable UI components, keep accessibility in mind. Ensure that your components are accessible to all users, including those with disabilities. Adhere to accessibility standards and guidelines, and consider using ARIA attributes and semantic HTML elements to enhance accessibility.

Another consideration is performance. While designing reusable components, be mindful of performance implications. Avoid unnecessary re-renders and optimize component rendering for smooth user experiences.

In summary, designing and building reusable UI components is a fundamental practice in web development that fosters efficiency, consistency, and maintainability. By identifying common patterns, designing flexible APIs, separating concerns, and providing comprehensive documentation, you can create components that empower developers and enhance the user experience. Through collaboration, version control, and adherence to accessibility and performance best practices, you can build a library of reusable components and establish a robust design system that elevates the quality of your web applications.

Chapter 10: Building a Single-Page Application

In the realm of web design and development, creating responsive layouts is an essential practice that ensures your websites and web applications look and function well on a variety of devices and screen sizes. With the proliferation of smartphones, tablets, and different desktop monitors, it's crucial to adapt your layouts to accommodate various screen dimensions. CSS media queries are a powerful tool in achieving responsive designs by allowing you to apply different styles and layouts based on the user's device or viewport size.

Responsive web design is a user-centered approach that prioritizes a seamless and enjoyable experience for all users, regardless of the device they are using. It acknowledges that people access websites and web apps from a wide range of devices and screen sizes, and it aims to provide an optimal presentation and functionality for each scenario.

Media queries are CSS rules that target specific conditions, such as screen width, height, or device orientation. These queries allow you to apply CSS styles selectively based on the characteristics of the user's device or viewport. By using media queries, you can create adaptive designs that automatically adjust to different screen sizes and orientations.

A fundamental use case of media queries is adjusting the layout or styling of a web page for smaller screens, such as those of smartphones and tablets. For example, you might want to make text larger and increase spacing between elements to enhance readability on smaller screens. You can achieve this by defining a media query that targets a maximum screen width and applies the desired styles accordingly.

Here's an example of a media query that adjusts font size and spacing for smaller screens:

cssCopy code

```
/* Default styles for larger screens */ body { font-size:
16px; line-height: 1.5; } /* Media query for screens
with a maximum width of 768 pixels (typical for tablets)
*/ @media screen and (max-width: 768px) { body {
font-size: 14px; line-height: 1.4; } }
```

In this example, the default styles apply to screens larger than 768 pixels wide, while the media query targets screens with a maximum width of 768 pixels or less. For those smaller screens, the font size and line height are reduced to improve readability.

Media queries are not limited to screen width; you can use them to target various characteristics, including screen height, device orientation (portrait or landscape), resolution, and more. This flexibility allows you to fine-tune your responsive designs to cater to different user experiences.

Another common use case for media queries is adjusting the layout of a webpage for both portrait and landscape orientations on mobile devices. For example, you might want to reposition elements or change the number of columns in a grid layout when the user switches between portrait and landscape modes.

Here's an example of a media query that adjusts a grid layout for landscape orientation:

cssCopy code

```
/* Default grid layout for portrait orientation */
.container { display: grid; grid-template-columns: 1fr;
} /* Media query for landscape orientation */ @media
screen and (min-width: 480px) and (orientation:
landscape) { .container { grid-template-columns: 1fr
1fr; } }
```

In this example, the default grid layout uses a single column for portrait orientation. When the device switches to landscape mode and has a minimum width of 480 pixels, the media query adjusts the layout to two columns for a more spacious presentation.

Media queries can also be used to create responsive navigation menus. For instance, on small screens, you might want to hide the regular horizontal navigation and replace it with a mobile-friendly, collapsible menu icon (commonly known as a "hamburger" menu).

Here's an example of a media query that hides the regular navigation and displays a mobile menu icon for small screens:

cssCopy code

```
/* Default styles for regular navigation */ .nav {
display: flex; } /* Media query for screens with a
maximum width of 768 pixels (typical for mobile
devices) */ @media screen and (max-width: 768px) {
/* Hide regular navigation */ .nav { display: none; } /*
```

Display mobile menu icon */ .mobile-menu-icon {
display: block; } }

In this example, the regular navigation is displayed by default, but it is hidden when the screen width falls below 768 pixels. At that point, the mobile menu icon becomes visible, allowing users to toggle the navigation menu.

Media queries are not limited to just adjusting styles; they can also be used to load different sets of CSS files or assets based on screen characteristics. This technique is commonly known as "responsive images," where you serve different image sizes or resolutions depending on the user's device capabilities.

For instance, you might serve smaller image files to mobile devices with limited bandwidth and larger images to desktop screens with higher resolution displays. This approach can significantly improve page load times and user experience.

Here's an example of a media query that loads different image sizes for different screen resolutions:

cssCopy code

```
/* Default image style */ .img { width: 100%; } /*
Media query for screens with a minimum pixel density
of 2 (typical for high-resolution displays) */ @media
screen and (min-resolution: 192dpi) { .img { /* Use
higher-resolution image */ background-image:
url('image@2x.jpg'); } }
```

In this example, the default image style applies to all screens. However, for screens with a minimum pixel density of 192 dots per inch (dpi), a higher-resolution image is loaded, enhancing the image quality for devices with high-resolution displays.

Media queries are a fundamental tool in responsive web design, allowing you to create flexible and adaptive layouts that cater to various device characteristics. By strategically applying media queries to your CSS, you can achieve a seamless user experience across different screen sizes, orientations, and device capabilities. Responsive design is no longer a nice-to-have feature; it's an essential practice in modern web development that ensures your content is accessible and visually appealing to users on a wide range of devices.

BOOK 3
ADVANCED JAVASCRIPT TECHNIQUES
MASTERING COMPLEX PROJECTS AND FRAMEWORKS

ROB BOTWRIGHT

Chapter 1: Advanced JavaScript Fundamentals Review

In the world of web development, architecting the structure of a Single-Page Application (SPA) is a pivotal step that lays the foundation for building modern and highly interactive web applications. SPA architecture revolves around the concept of delivering a seamless user experience by loading a single HTML page and dynamically updating its content without the need for full-page reloads. To achieve this, careful planning and organization of the SPA's structure are essential.

At the core of SPA architecture is the idea of client-side routing. In traditional multi-page applications, routing is handled on the server, where different URLs correspond to different HTML pages. In a SPA, routing is managed on the client side, meaning that when users click on links or enter URLs, the SPA decides which content to display without making a request to the server. This results in faster and more responsive user interfaces.

To implement client-side routing in a SPA, developers commonly use libraries or frameworks like React Router, Vue Router, or Angular Router. These tools provide the means to define routes, map them to specific components, and handle navigation without causing full-page reloads. By organizing routes, you can ensure that each URL corresponds to a particular view or page within your SPA.

A typical SPA structure consists of various components, each responsible for rendering a specific part of the user interface. Components can range from simple elements like buttons and input fields to complex views like user profiles or product listings. Organizing these components in a structured and modular way is crucial for maintaining a manageable codebase.

One common architectural pattern used in SPAs is the component-based architecture. This approach encourages developers to break down the user interface into reusable, self-contained components. Each component should have a single responsibility and encapsulate both its logic and presentation.

For example, you might have separate components for a navigation bar, product list, and user profile. These components can be reused throughout the application, promoting consistency and reducing code duplication.

In addition to components, managing state is a critical aspect of SPA architecture. State refers to the data that your application uses to render views and respond to user interactions. In a SPA, state management can be complex, as the user can navigate between different views while preserving certain pieces of data.

State management libraries like Redux (for React) or Vuex (for Vue.js) provide a centralized way to manage and share state across components. They offer mechanisms for updating state, notifying components of changes, and ensuring that data remains consistent throughout the application.

Another consideration when architecting SPAs is lazy loading. As SPAs can grow in complexity, loading all JavaScript and CSS assets upfront can lead to longer initial load times. Lazy loading involves loading assets (such as scripts or styles) only when they are needed, typically as the user navigates to a particular view or route. This technique helps optimize performance by reducing the initial load size and prioritizing resources based on user interactions.

Webpack, a popular module bundler, supports code splitting and lazy loading out of the box. Using code splitting, you can split your JavaScript bundles into smaller chunks, allowing you to load only the necessary code for each route or view. This leads to a more efficient use of resources and a faster loading experience for users.

SPA architecture also raises the question of API integration. SPAs often need to interact with server-side APIs to fetch and update data. Architecting this interaction involves designing a clean and consistent API layer that abstracts away the details of making HTTP requests.

Many SPAs use libraries like Axios or the fetch API to handle HTTP requests. By encapsulating API calls within dedicated services or modules, you can ensure that data fetching and manipulation are organized and reusable. Additionally, error handling and authentication logic can be centralized within the API layer, promoting consistency across the application.

Security is another crucial aspect of SPA architecture. As much of the application's functionality resides on the client side, it's essential to secure your SPA against common web vulnerabilities, such as Cross-Site Scripting (XSS) and Cross-Site Request Forgery (CSRF). Implementing security best practices and regularly updating dependencies are key steps in safeguarding your SPA.

To optimize the performance of your SPA, consider techniques like code splitting, minification, and compression to reduce file sizes. Utilize browser caching and implement client-side caching strategies to store and reuse data where appropriate. These optimizations can significantly enhance the loading speed and responsiveness of your SPA.

Testing is an integral part of SPA architecture. Comprehensive testing helps identify and address issues early in the development process, ensuring a reliable and bug-free application. Unit tests, integration tests, and end-to-end tests can be employed to cover different aspects of your SPA, from individual components to user interactions.

Continuous integration (CI) and continuous deployment (CD) pipelines can automate the testing and deployment process, ensuring that changes are thoroughly tested before being deployed to production.

Lastly, documentation is paramount in SPA architecture. Documenting the structure of your SPA, the purpose of components, and the available routes and APIs aids in onboarding new team members and maintaining the application over time. Clear and up-to-date documentation fosters collaboration and ensures that all developers have a shared understanding of the SPA's architecture and design.

In summary, architecting the structure of a Single-Page Application (SPA) is a crucial step in developing modern and responsive web applications. By focusing on client-side routing, component-based architecture, state management, lazy loading, API integration, security, performance optimization, testing, and documentation, you can create a robust and maintainable SPA. SPAs offer a user-centric experience, providing fast and seamless interactions that cater to today's web users across various devices and screen sizes.

In the world of JavaScript programming, understanding data types and objects is fundamental to harnessing the full power of the language. JavaScript is a dynamically typed language, meaning that variables can hold values of different types, and these types can change during the execution of a program. This flexibility allows developers to create versatile and dynamic applications. Let's start by exploring JavaScript's basic data types. The most fundamental data types in JavaScript are numbers, strings, booleans, undefined, and null. Numbers can be integers or floating-point values, allowing for precise mathematical operations. Strings represent text and can be enclosed in single or double quotes. Booleans have only two possible values: true and false. Undefined is a special value indicating that a variable has been declared but has not yet been assigned a value. Null is another special value that represents the intentional absence of any object value.

Variables in JavaScript can be declared using the var, let, or const keywords. var is the oldest and most flexible, but it has some scoping quirks that can lead to unexpected behavior. let and const were introduced in ECMAScript 2015 (ES6) and have block-level scoping, making them more predictable and safer to use.

Objects are a crucial concept in JavaScript, and they can be thought of as collections of key-value pairs. Objects allow you to represent complex data structures and organize related data. In JavaScript, objects are defined using curly braces {} and can contain properties and methods.

Properties in JavaScript objects are key-value pairs where the key is a string (or a Symbol) and the value can be of any data type. For example, you can create an object representing a person with properties like "name," "age," and "city."

javascriptCopy code

```
const person = { name: "John Doe", age: 30, city: "New York", };
```

To access the values of object properties, you can use dot notation or square bracket notation. For example, person.name and person["name"] both yield the value "John Doe."

JavaScript also provides a way to define methods on objects. Methods are simply functions stored as object properties. Here's an example of an object with a method:

javascriptCopy code

```
const person = { name: "John Doe", age: 30, sayHello: function () { console.log(`Hello, my name is ${this.name}.`); }, };
```

You can call the sayHello method of the person object by using dot notation: person.sayHello().

In addition to generic objects, JavaScript has several built-in objects that provide specialized functionality. One of the most commonly used built-in objects is the Array object. Arrays are ordered collections of values, and you can access their elements using numerical indices.

javascriptCopy code

```
const fruits = ["apple", "banana", "cherry"];
console.log(fruits[0]); // "apple"
```

Arrays also come with a variety of methods for manipulating and iterating over their elements, making them powerful data structures for many scenarios.

Another important built-in object is the Date object, which allows you to work with dates and times. You can create a Date object representing the current date and time or a specific date by providing year, month, day, and other parameters.

javascriptCopy code

```
const currentDate = new Date();
console.log(currentDate); const christmas2023 = new Date(2023, 11, 25); console.log(christmas2023);
```

The Date object provides methods for retrieving and manipulating various components of dates and times, such as the year, month, day, hours, minutes, and seconds.

Functions are first-class citizens in JavaScript, which means they can be assigned to variables, passed as arguments to other functions, and returned as values from functions. This flexibility enables powerful functional programming paradigms and allows you to create higher-order functions that operate on other functions.

Here's an example of a simple higher-order function that takes a function as an argument and executes it:

```javascript
javascriptCopy code
function executeFunction(func) { func(); } function
sayHello() { console.log("Hello, world!"); }
executeFunction(sayHello);
```

JavaScript also supports anonymous functions, which are functions without names. You can define them inline, and they are often used as callbacks or for one-time use.

```javascript
javascriptCopy code
const add = function (a, b) { return a + b; }; const
result = add(5, 3); console.log(result); // 8
```

Arrow functions, introduced in ES6, provide a concise syntax for defining functions, especially when they have a single statement.

```javascript
javascriptCopy code
const square = (x) => x * x; console.log(square(4));
// 16
```

JavaScript also has a concept called closures. A closure is a function that retains access to variables from its containing lexical scope even after that scope has finished executing. Closures are often used to create private variables and encapsulate functionality.

Here's an example of a closure:

```javascript
javascriptCopy code
function createCounter() { let count = 0; return
function () { count++; console.log(count); }; } const
counter = createCounter(); counter(); // 1 counter();
// 2
```

In this example, the inner function maintains access to the count variable even though the createCounter function has finished executing.

Another essential aspect of JavaScript's data types is type coercion. Type coercion is the automatic conversion of values from one data type to another by JavaScript. Understanding how type coercion works is crucial to avoid unexpected behavior in your code.

For example, JavaScript will try to convert values to the same type when performing operations. This can lead to unexpected results if you're not aware of how the coercion rules work.

javascriptCopy code

```
console.log("5" + 5); // "55" (string concatenation)
console.log("5" - 2); // 3 (numeric subtraction)
```

To avoid surprises, it's a good practice to use explicit type conversion functions like parseInt() and parseFloat() when needed.

In summary, a deep dive into JavaScript data types and objects is essential for any developer working with the language. Understanding the basic data types, objects, properties, methods, and functions is the foundation for building robust and efficient JavaScript applications. With this knowledge, you can create dynamic, versatile, and powerful web applications that cater to a wide range of use cases and user interactions.

In the world of software design and object-oriented programming, the creation of objects plays a pivotal role in building applications. One of the fundamental questions developers face is how to create and manage objects efficiently, ensuring that they meet the requirements of the application while maintaining a clean and organized codebase. To address this challenge, software design patterns offer tried-and-tested solutions. Two commonly used design patterns for object creation are the Singleton and Factory patterns.

The Singleton pattern is a creational pattern that restricts the instantiation of a class to a single instance. In essence, it ensures that there's only one instance of a particular class, regardless of how many times you request that instance. This can be beneficial in scenarios where having multiple instances of a class would lead to unexpected behavior or resource waste.

The Singleton pattern is typically implemented by defining a private static variable within the class, which holds the single instance of the class. A private constructor is also defined to prevent external instantiation. A public static method is then provided to access the single instance, and this method initializes the instance if it doesn't exist or returns the existing instance.

Here's a simple example of a Singleton pattern in JavaScript:

javascriptCopy code

```
class Singleton { constructor() { if
(!Singleton.instance) { Singleton.instance = this; }
return Singleton.instance; } }
```

In this example, the Singleton class ensures that there's only one instance of itself. Any attempts to create multiple instances will return the same instance.

The Singleton pattern is useful in situations where you want to centralize control over resources, such as database connections, configuration settings, or logging services. By having a single instance, you can ensure that these resources are managed efficiently and consistently throughout your application.

On the other hand, the Factory pattern is a creational pattern that provides an interface for creating objects but allows subclasses to alter the type of objects that will be created. This pattern is particularly useful when you have multiple related classes with a common base class, and you want to delegate the responsibility of object creation to subclasses.

The Factory pattern involves defining a factory class or method that encapsulates the object creation logic. This factory class or method can take parameters and decide which concrete class to instantiate based on those parameters.

Here's a simple example of a Factory pattern in JavaScript:

javascriptCopy code

```
class AnimalFactory { createAnimal(type) { switch
(type) { case "cat": return new Cat(); case "dog":
return new Dog(); default: throw new Error("Invalid
animal type"); } } } class Cat { speak() {
console.log("Meow!"); } } class Dog { speak() {
console.log("Woof!"); } }
```

In this example, the AnimalFactory class is responsible for creating different types of animals based on the provided type parameter. By using a factory, you can abstract away the object creation process and make it more flexible.

The Factory pattern is beneficial when you need to decouple the client code from the concrete classes it creates. It allows you to switch between different implementations of related classes without affecting the client code. For example, you could easily change the AnimalFactory to create different subclasses of animals without changing the code that uses the factory.

While the Singleton and Factory patterns address different aspects of object creation, they share common goals of promoting efficient object management and maintaining clean and organized code.

When to use the Singleton pattern:

Use the Singleton pattern when you need to ensure that a class has only one instance, such as managing a shared resource or configuration settings.

It can also be helpful when you want to provide a single point of access to a particular service or functionality.

When to use the Factory pattern:

Use the Factory pattern when you want to delegate the responsibility of object creation to subclasses or when you need to create objects based on specific conditions or parameters.

It's particularly useful in scenarios where you have multiple related classes with a common interface or base class.

Both patterns have their strengths and weaknesses, and the choice between them depends on the specific requirements of your application. The Singleton pattern enforces a single instance but can sometimes lead to tight coupling in your code. The Factory pattern, on the other hand, offers more flexibility in object creation but can be more complex to implement.

In summary, the Singleton and Factory patterns are valuable tools in the developer's toolbox for creating objects wisely in software applications. By carefully considering when and how to apply these patterns, you can design more maintainable, flexible, and efficient code that meets the needs of your projects.

Chapter 3: Effective Debugging Strategies

In the world of web development, debugging is an essential skill, and mastering browser Developer Tools can significantly enhance your efficiency and effectiveness as a developer. Developer Tools, often referred to as DevTools, are built-in features in modern web browsers that allow you to inspect and manipulate web pages, as well as debug JavaScript, CSS, and other web technologies. Learning how to make the most of these tools is a valuable investment in your development workflow.

One of the first steps in mastering DevTools is familiarizing yourself with how to open them. In most browsers, you can access DevTools by right-clicking on a web page element and selecting "Inspect" or by pressing the F12 key or Ctrl+Shift+I (Cmd+Option+I on Mac). Once DevTools are open, you'll see a variety of tabs and panels that provide different functionalities.

The "Elements" panel is one of the most commonly used panels in DevTools. It allows you to inspect and manipulate the HTML and CSS of a web page in real-time. You can click on elements in the panel to highlight them on the page, and you can modify the HTML and CSS directly to see how it affects the rendering of the page. This panel is invaluable for diagnosing and fixing layout and styling issues.

The "Console" panel is where you can interact with JavaScript running on the page. You can type JavaScript expressions and commands, and the console will execute them. It's an excellent place for debugging and testing JavaScript code. The console also displays error messages and warnings, helping you identify and resolve issues in your code.

When debugging JavaScript, the "Sources" panel is your best friend. It allows you to set breakpoints in your code, inspect variables, step through code execution, and watch expressions. These features are crucial for understanding how your JavaScript code is behaving and identifying the root causes of bugs. You can even blackbox third-party scripts to exclude them from debugging sessions if they are not relevant to your code.

The "Network" panel is useful for monitoring network requests made by your web page. It shows you details about each request, including headers, response data, and timing. This panel is valuable for diagnosing issues related to data retrieval, API calls, and network performance. You can also simulate different network conditions to test how your application behaves in slow or offline scenarios.

For diagnosing and optimizing the performance of your web page, the "Performance" and "Audits" panels are essential. The "Performance" panel records and analyzes the runtime performance of your page, including JavaScript execution, rendering, and network activity. It helps you pinpoint performance bottlenecks and optimize your code. The "Audits" panel provides automated checks and recommendations for improving page speed, accessibility, and best practices.

The "Application" panel allows you to inspect and manipulate browser storage, such as cookies, local storage, and indexedDB. You can view, edit, and delete data stored by your web page. This panel is especially useful when working with client-side data storage and user authentication.

In addition to these core panels, DevTools also offer features like "Device Mode" for responsive design testing, "Security" for checking security-related issues, and "Animations" for debugging CSS animations and transitions. Each of these panels and features serves a specific purpose in the development and debugging process.

One of the key advantages of using DevTools is the ability to set breakpoints in your JavaScript code. Breakpoints allow you to pause the execution of your code at specific lines or functions, giving you the opportunity to inspect variables and step through the code to understand its flow. This is invaluable for identifying logic errors and unexpected behavior in your JavaScript.

Conditional breakpoints take this a step further by allowing you to specify conditions under which the breakpoint should be triggered. For example, you can set a breakpoint to trigger only when a certain variable reaches a specific value. This feature is incredibly useful for debugging complex scenarios where you want to focus on specific conditions.

Another powerful tool in DevTools is the "Console" panel, which not only displays error messages but also allows you to log information, warnings, and custom messages from your JavaScript code. By strategically adding logging statements to your code, you can gain insights into the state of your application and track the flow of data. The ability to inspect objects and variables in the console is particularly helpful for understanding how data changes over time.

The "Sources" panel provides a rich set of debugging features, including the ability to set breakpoints, step through code execution, and watch expressions. You can also blackbox third-party scripts to exclude them from debugging sessions, which can be helpful when working with complex applications that rely on external libraries.

When debugging asynchronous code, DevTools offers a dedicated "Async" mode in the "Sources" panel. This mode allows you to track the flow of asynchronous operations, such as promises and async/await functions, making it easier to understand and debug asynchronous code.

In addition to traditional breakpoints, DevTools supports "DOM breakpoints" that allow you to pause execution when specific DOM events occur. This is useful for debugging interactions with the DOM, such as click events, form submissions, or changes to specific elements. By setting DOM breakpoints, you can gain insights into how user interactions trigger code execution.

DevTools also provides a feature called "Live Expressions," which allows you to create custom expressions that are continuously evaluated as you interact with the page. Live Expressions are handy for monitoring specific variables or properties in real-time without the need for manual console logging.

In summary, mastering browser Developer Tools is a valuable skill for web developers. These tools offer a comprehensive set of features for inspecting, debugging, and optimizing web pages and applications. By becoming proficient in the use of DevTools panels like "Elements," "Console," "Sources," "Network," "Performance," and "Audits," you can streamline your development workflow, diagnose and fix issues more efficiently, and create web experiences that are faster, more reliable, and user-friendly.

Chapter 4: Working with JavaScript Frameworks

Debugging asynchronous code can be challenging, as it involves code that doesn't execute sequentially, making it harder to predict and control the flow of execution. Asynchronous code often relies on callbacks, promises, and async/await syntax to handle operations that take time, such as network requests or file reading. Understanding how to effectively debug asynchronous code is a crucial skill for any developer.

One of the most common tools for debugging asynchronous code is the browser's developer console. The console allows you to log messages, errors, and the values of variables, helping you understand the flow of your asynchronous code. By strategically placing console.log statements at different points in your code, you can track the order of execution and identify any unexpected behavior.

When debugging asynchronous code, it's essential to understand the concept of a callback function. Callback functions are functions that are passed as arguments to other functions and are executed when a specific event or condition occurs. They are prevalent in JavaScript, especially when working with asynchronous operations.

To debug asynchronous code with callbacks, you can place console.log statements inside your callback functions. For example, if you're handling an AJAX request with a callback function, you can log the response data or any errors inside the callback to see what's happening.
javascriptCopy code

```javascript
fetch("https://api.example.com/data").then((response)
=> { if (!response.ok) { console.error("Network
response was not ok"); return; } return response.json();
}).then((data) => { console.log("Data received:", data);
}) .catch((error) => { console.error("Error fetching
data:", error); });
```

In this example, we use console.log and console.error to
log the flow of execution and any errors that occur during
the AJAX request.

Another valuable technique for debugging asynchronous
code is using breakpoints. You can set breakpoints in your
code using your browser's developer tools or an
integrated development environment (IDE). When the
code execution reaches a breakpoint, it pauses, allowing
you to inspect variables and the call stack.

By setting breakpoints strategically in your asynchronous
code, you can observe how different parts of your code
interact and identify any issues that may arise. You can
also step through the code one line at a time to
understand the sequence of operations.

Promises are a powerful tool for handling asynchronous
operations in a more structured way. They provide a clean
and organized way to work with asynchronous code,
making it easier to handle success and error cases.

When debugging code that uses promises, it's essential to
use the .then() and .catch() methods effectively. You can
place console.log statements inside these methods to
track the flow of execution and handle any errors that
occur.

javascriptCopy code

```javascript
function fetchData() {
fetch("https://api.example.com/data").then((response)
=> { if (!response.ok) { console.error("Network
response was not ok"); throw new Error("Network
response was not ok"); } return response.json(); })
.then((data) => { console.log("Data received:", data); })
.catch((error) => { console.error("Error fetching data:",
error); }); } fetchData();
```

In this example, we use .then() to handle the response data and .catch() to catch and handle any errors. By logging messages and errors within these methods, you can gain insight into how your promise-based asynchronous code behaves.

Async/await is a more recent addition to JavaScript that simplifies working with promises. It allows you to write asynchronous code in a more synchronous style, making it easier to read and understand. When debugging async/await code, you can use similar techniques as with promises.

javascriptCopy code

```javascript
async function fetchData() { try { const response =
await fetch("https://api.example.com/data"); if
(!response.ok) { console.error("Network response was
not ok"); throw new Error("Network response was not
ok"); } const data = await response.json();
console.log("Data received:", data); } catch (error) {
console.error("Error fetching data:", error); } }
fetchData();
```

In this example, we use try/catch to handle errors, and we log messages within the async function to track the flow of execution.

When debugging asynchronous code, it's crucial to pay attention to the call stack and the order of function calls. The call stack displays the current function calls, helping you understand the sequence of execution.

In addition to the call stack, you can also use the "Async" tab in your browser's developer tools to trace the flow of asynchronous operations. This tab provides a visual representation of async/await code execution, making it easier to identify where code pauses and resumes.

Another useful debugging technique for asynchronous code is using breakpoints with conditional statements. You can set breakpoints that only trigger when a specific condition is met. This can be helpful when you want to inspect variables or step through code only in specific scenarios.

In summary, debugging asynchronous code and promises in JavaScript requires a combination of techniques. Using console.log, console.error, and breakpoints strategically can help you understand the flow of execution and identify issues. Understanding callback functions, promises, and async/await syntax is essential for working with asynchronous code effectively. With practice and experience, you can become proficient at debugging asynchronous code and building more reliable and responsive web applications.

Chapter 5: React in Depth: Components and State Management

Selecting the right JavaScript framework for your project is a crucial decision that can significantly impact the success and maintainability of your application. Frameworks play a pivotal role in web development by providing a structured foundation for building complex and interactive web applications. With numerous JavaScript frameworks available, each offering unique features and capabilities, it's essential to make an informed choice based on your project's specific requirements and constraints.

One of the first considerations when choosing a JavaScript framework is the project's scope and complexity. Different frameworks cater to various project sizes and objectives. For smaller projects or simple websites, you might opt for a lightweight library like React or Vue.js. These libraries focus on the view layer and offer flexibility for integrating with other tools and libraries. On the other hand, for large-scale applications with extensive functionality and complex data management, a full-fledged framework like Angular or Ember.js may be more suitable. These frameworks provide a comprehensive set of features, including routing, state management, and testing, out of the box.

Another critical factor to consider is the skill set of your development team. If your team is already experienced with a particular framework, it often makes sense to leverage that expertise. Choosing a framework that aligns with your team's knowledge can lead to faster development and better code quality. However, if you're starting from scratch or have a team with diverse skills, it's worth evaluating which framework aligns best with your project's requirements and learning curve.

Performance is a significant consideration when selecting a JavaScript framework. Different frameworks have varying performance characteristics, and the impact on your application can be substantial. If your project prioritizes high performance and responsiveness, you may need to conduct benchmarking tests and performance profiling to determine which framework meets your needs. In some cases, optimizing the performance of a chosen framework through code splitting, lazy loading, or other techniques may be necessary.

The ecosystem and community support surrounding a framework can also influence your decision. A strong and active community can provide valuable resources, such as documentation, tutorials, and third-party libraries. It can also offer support through forums, discussions, and contributions to the framework itself. Consider whether the framework you're considering has a vibrant community that can assist with problem-solving and staying up-to-date with best practices.

Compatibility with other tools and technologies in your tech stack is crucial. Ensure that the framework integrates smoothly with your chosen build tools, package managers, and other libraries. For example, if you're using a specific state management library or a CSS preprocessor, verify that your chosen framework supports or can be easily integrated with these technologies.

The architecture and design philosophy of a framework play a significant role in how you develop and maintain your application. Some frameworks, like React, embrace a component-based architecture, while others, like Angular, follow a more opinionated structure. Consider whether the framework aligns with your project's design principles and whether its conventions match your team's coding style and preferences. Additionally, evaluate the framework's maintainability and long-term support. Check its release history and community-driven updates to ensure that it remains actively maintained and receives security patches and improvements.

One of the most critical aspects of choosing a JavaScript framework is evaluating its documentation and learning resources. Clear and comprehensive documentation is essential for onboarding new team members and resolving issues quickly. Explore the framework's official documentation to assess its quality and availability. Additionally, look for online tutorials, courses, and books related to the framework to gauge the availability of learning materials.

Consider the licensing and legal implications of using a particular framework. Most JavaScript frameworks are open-source and released under permissive licenses like MIT or Apache 2.0, which allows for commercial and non-commercial use. However, it's essential to review the licensing terms and ensure that they align with your project's legal requirements and constraints.

Another crucial factor is the framework's flexibility and extensibility. Evaluate whether the framework can adapt to your project's unique needs and whether it supports custom extensions and plugins. Frameworks that provide a rich ecosystem of third-party packages and extensions can save development time and effort.

Community and industry trends can also influence your framework choice. Stay informed about the latest developments in the JavaScript ecosystem and assess whether a framework is gaining or losing popularity. While a framework's popularity alone should not drive your decision, it can provide insights into its adoption and long-term viability.

Consider the long-term perspective of your project. Think about how easy it will be to maintain and update your application over time. Some frameworks may become less relevant or undergo significant changes, leading to migration challenges. Assess the framework's track record in terms of backward compatibility and how well it has handled major updates in the past.

When making your decision, it's beneficial to conduct a proof of concept or a small pilot project using the selected framework. This allows your team to gain hands-on experience and assess whether the framework meets your project's needs in practice. Additionally, it helps identify any potential roadblocks or challenges early in the development process.

Lastly, consider the scalability of your project. Evaluate whether the chosen framework can grow with your application as it evolves. Some frameworks are better suited for small to medium-sized projects, while others are designed to handle the complexities of enterprise-level applications. Scalability encompasses not only performance but also the ability to maintain code quality and developer productivity as the project expands.

In summary, choosing the right JavaScript framework for your project is a critical decision that requires careful consideration of various factors. Assess the project's scope, your team's expertise, performance requirements, community support, compatibility with other tools, architectural alignment, documentation quality, legal considerations, flexibility, industry trends, and long-term maintainability. Conduct a proof of concept to validate your choice and ensure that the framework can meet the scalability needs of your project. By making an informed decision, you can set your project up for success and create a robust and maintainable web application.

Chapter 6: Angular Mastery: Dependency Injection and Services

Understanding the component lifecycle is essential for optimizing the performance of your web applications built with JavaScript frameworks such as React, Angular, or Vue.js. In these frameworks, components are the building blocks of your application's user interface, and they have a lifecycle that determines when they are created, updated, and destroyed. By gaining insight into this lifecycle and employing optimization techniques, you can create web applications that are more responsive and efficient.

The component lifecycle typically consists of several phases, starting with the creation phase. During the creation phase, a component is instantiated, and its constructor is called. This is where you can initialize component-specific data, set up event listeners, and perform other one-time setup tasks. Understanding the order of execution of the constructor and component-specific methods is crucial for effective initialization.

After the constructor is executed, the component enters the "render" phase. In this phase, the component generates a virtual representation of its user interface based on its current state and props. This virtual representation is then used to update the actual DOM elements. Efficient rendering is vital for achieving good performance, as rendering is often a frequent operation in web applications.

One optimization technique during the rendering phase is to minimize the number of re-renders. Components should only re-render when their state or props change. You can achieve this by implementing shouldComponentUpdate (in React), ngOnChanges (in Angular), or the equivalent mechanism in your chosen framework. These methods allow you to specify under which conditions a component should update. By carefully managing updates, you reduce unnecessary rendering, improving performance.

In addition to minimizing re-renders, it's essential to optimize the rendering process itself. Frameworks like React use a virtual DOM to efficiently update the actual DOM. The virtual DOM is a lightweight representation of the actual DOM, and changes are first applied to the virtual DOM before being synchronized with the real DOM. This diffing process ensures that only the necessary changes are made to the DOM, reducing the performance overhead.

When optimizing rendering, consider using techniques like memoization and memoized selectors. Memoization involves caching the results of expensive calculations and returning the cached result when the same input is encountered again. Memoized selectors, popularized by libraries like Reselect, allow you to compute derived data efficiently and avoid recomputation when the component re-renders.

The next phase in the component lifecycle is the "componentDidMount" (in React) or "ngAfterViewInit" (in Angular) phase. During this phase, the component has been rendered to the DOM, and you can perform tasks that require access to the DOM, such as setting up third-party libraries, fetching data from APIs, or initializing animations. However, be cautious with time-consuming operations in this phase, as they can block the main thread and affect the application's responsiveness.

To mitigate potential performance issues in the "componentDidMount" or "ngAfterViewInit" phase, consider asynchronous operations and lazy loading. Perform asynchronous tasks like data fetching or image loading in a non-blocking manner using Promises or observables. Additionally, employ techniques like code splitting to load only the necessary code for specific routes or components, reducing the initial load time.

As your component interacts with the user and receives new data or user input, it enters the "update" phase. In this phase, the component re-renders when its state or props change. Efficiently handling updates is crucial for maintaining a responsive user interface.

To optimize updates, avoid direct mutation of state or props. In many frameworks, changes to state or props trigger re-renders. Immutable data structures or immutable patterns can help ensure that changes to data result in new objects rather than modifying existing ones. This helps maintain the purity of the rendering process and simplifies debugging.

Another optimization technique for updates is using PureComponent or shouldComponentUpdate (in React) or the equivalent in other frameworks. These mechanisms allow you to control when a component should update. By comparing the previous and current state or props and determining whether a re-render is necessary, you can prevent unnecessary rendering and improve performance.

In the context of Angular, employing OnPush change detection strategy can be beneficial. This strategy makes components update only when their inputs change or when triggered manually, reducing the number of change detection cycles.

Performance optimization extends beyond the component itself to include the component's children. When optimizing a component that renders a list of items, consider implementing virtualization. Virtualization techniques, such as windowing or infinite scrolling, render only a subset of the list at a time, significantly reducing the DOM elements and rendering workload. This approach is especially effective for long lists or grids.= Another crucial aspect of performance optimization is memory management. In long-running applications, memory leaks can occur if references to objects are not properly cleaned up when components are unmounted or disposed of. To address this, ensure that event listeners, timers, and subscriptions are properly removed when a component is no longer needed.

Frameworks often provide lifecycle hooks or mechanisms for cleaning up resources in the "componentWillUnmount" (in React) or "ngOnDestroy" (in Angular) phase. Use these hooks to release resources and prevent memory leaks. Additionally, consider using tools like Chrome DevTools or memory profilers to identify and address memory-related issues.

Optimizing component performance is an ongoing process that requires monitoring and profiling. Performance bottlenecks can vary depending on the complexity of your application, so regularly profiling and benchmarking your components is essential to identifying and addressing issues.

Lastly, consider browser-specific optimizations, such as leveraging the browser's requestAnimationFrame API for smooth animations and transitions. Browser dev tools offer performance profiling and auditing tools to help you identify and address performance bottlenecks specific to your application.

In summary, component lifecycle and performance optimization are critical aspects of developing efficient and responsive web applications. Understanding the component lifecycle phases, minimizing re-renders, optimizing rendering, and handling updates efficiently are key techniques for improving component performance. Additionally, consider optimizations related to data handling, memory management, and browser-specific features to create web applications that offer a smooth and performant user experience.

Chapter 7: Vue.js Advanced Techniques: Custom Directives and Vuex

Angular's dependency injection (DI) is a fundamental concept that plays a central role in developing scalable and maintainable applications. At its core, DI is a design pattern that helps manage the dependencies of components and services within an Angular application. It promotes code reusability, testability, and separation of concerns, making it a valuable tool for building complex web applications.

In Angular, DI is implemented through the Dependency Injection Container, which is responsible for creating and managing instances of various classes and services. The container maintains a registry of providers, which are responsible for instantiating and configuring objects. Providers define how objects are created and injected into components, services, or other objects. There are different types of providers in Angular, such as value providers, class providers, and factory providers, each serving specific purposes. Value providers supply a constant value, class providers create instances of a class, and factory providers invoke a factory function to create objects.

One of the key benefits of DI is that it promotes the use of interfaces and abstractions. Instead of directly referencing concrete implementations, components and services depend on abstractions, making it easier to swap out implementations or introduce mock objects for testing. This separation of concerns allows for more modular and maintainable code.

In Angular, DI is enabled by default, meaning that components, services, and other objects can receive their dependencies as constructor parameters. When a component or service is instantiated, Angular's DI system examines its constructor signature to determine what dependencies it needs and provides them automatically.

For example, consider a service that fetches data from a remote server. Instead of directly creating an instance of this service within a component, you can specify the service as a constructor parameter. Angular's DI system will then create and inject an instance of the service when the component is instantiated.

typescriptCopy code

```typescript
import { Injectable } from '@angular/core';
@Injectable() export class DataService { // Service implementation... }
```

typescriptCopy code

```typescript
import { Component } from '@angular/core'; import { DataService } from './data.service'; @Component({ selector: 'app-example', template: '<p>Data: {{ data }}</p>', }) export class ExampleComponent { constructor(private dataService: DataService) {} private data: any; ngOnInit() { this.data = this.dataService.getData(); } }
```

In this example, the DataService is marked with @Injectable, indicating that it can be injected into other components or services. The ExampleComponent constructor accepts a parameter of type DataService, and Angular's DI system provides an instance of DataService when creating an instance of ExampleComponent.

DI in Angular is not limited to services; it can be used with any class or object that has dependencies. This includes components, other services, and even Angular modules themselves.

In addition to constructor injection, Angular also supports property and method injection. Property injection involves using the @Inject decorator to specify a dependency directly on a property. Method injection is less common and typically involves calling a method to explicitly provide a dependency.

While constructor injection is the most common and recommended approach in Angular, property and method injection can be useful in certain scenarios.

Angular's DI system also supports hierarchical injection. This means that Angular maintains a hierarchy of injectors, and each component has its own injector. When a component requests a dependency, Angular first checks its own injector, and if the dependency is not found, it looks up the hierarchy until it finds a provider or reaches the root injector. This mechanism allows for more fine-grained control over the scope and lifetime of dependencies.

The root injector is created when the Angular application starts and serves as the top-level injector for the entire application. It typically provides global services and dependencies that should be available throughout the application.

Providers play a crucial role in configuring how dependencies are resolved. In Angular, you can provide dependencies at different levels, such as at the component level, the module level, or globally. This flexibility allows you to control the scope and lifetime of dependencies based on your application's needs.

For example, you can provide a service at the component level, ensuring that each instance of the component receives its own unique instance of the service. Alternatively, you can provide a service at the module level, making it available to all components within that module. Global providers, often configured in the root module, ensure that a single instance of a service is shared across the entire application.

When defining providers, you can specify various options, including the useClass, useValue, useFactory, and useExisting properties. These options allow you to control how dependencies are created and configured.

One common use case for providers is configuring services to use different implementations in different environments. For example, during development, you might want to use a mock service for testing purposes, while in production, you use the actual service that communicates with a server. By configuring providers appropriately, you can achieve this without changing the consuming components.

Angular also provides a powerful feature known as "InjectionToken." An InjectionToken is a special kind of token that can be used to define dependencies that do not have a class-based representation. This is especially useful when injecting configuration values or non-class dependencies into components and services.

typescriptCopy code

```
import { InjectionToken } from '@angular/core';
export const API_URL = new InjectionToken<string>('apiUrl'); // In a module's providers array: { provide: API_URL, useValue: 'https://api.example.com', }
```

In this example, we define an InjectionToken called API_URL and provide a value for it in a module's providers array. This allows us to inject the API_URL token into components or services to access the configured API URL without needing a class-based dependency.

Overall, understanding Angular's dependency injection system is essential for building maintainable, testable, and scalable applications. It encourages the use of abstractions, promotes modular code, and allows for flexible configuration of dependencies. By leveraging DI and providers effectively, you can design robust and adaptable Angular applications.

Custom Vue.js directives empower you to extend the functionality of your Vue.js applications by introducing new, reusable, and declarative behavior to your components. Vue.js, a popular JavaScript framework, provides a set of built-in directives like v-if, v-for, and v-bind that allow you to control the rendering and behavior of your templates. However, in many cases, you may find the need to create your own directives to encapsulate specific functionality or enhance the readability of your templates.

Custom directives in Vue.js are a powerful tool that enables you to encapsulate complex or repetitive DOM manipulations and interactions into simple, declarative directives. By creating custom directives, you can promote code reuse, enhance maintainability, and improve the overall readability of your Vue components.

A Vue.js directive is essentially a special token in the markup that tells the framework to do something to a DOM element or a component. Directives are prefixed with the v- prefix to indicate that they are special attributes provided by Vue.js. For example, v-if is a built-in directive that controls the conditional rendering of an element based on a provided condition.

To create a custom directive in Vue.js, you use the Vue.directive method to register it globally or locally within a component. Global directives are available throughout your application, while local directives are specific to the component in which they are defined.

Custom directives consist of two main functions: bind and update. The bind function is called once when the directive is first bound to an element, allowing you to perform any initial setup or configuration. The update function is called whenever the bound element or component updates, allowing you to react to changes and apply any necessary behavior.

For example, let's create a simple custom directive that highlights an element when the mouse hovers over it. We'll name this directive v-highlight:

javascriptCopy code

```
// Register a global custom directive called `v-highlight`
Vue.directive('highlight', { // bind function bind(el,
binding) { // Set the element's background color to the
specified value when bound el.style.backgroundColor
= binding.value; }, // update function update(el,
binding) { // Change the background color when the
value changes el.style.backgroundColor =
binding.value; }, });
```

In this example, we register a global custom directive called v-highlight using Vue.directive. The directive has a bind function that sets the background color of the element to the specified value when it's initially bound. The update function is called whenever the value of the directive changes, allowing us to update the background color dynamically.

To use this custom directive in a Vue component template, you can simply add it as an attribute to an element with the v-prefix:

htmlCopy code

```
<template> <div> <p v-highlight="'yellow'">Hover me
to highlight</p> </div> </template>
```

In this template, we apply the v-highlight directive to a paragraph element and pass the color 'yellow' as its value. When the mouse hovers over the paragraph, it will be highlighted in yellow, as defined by our custom directive.

Custom directives can also accept arguments and modifiers. Arguments allow you to pass additional values to the directive, while modifiers provide a way to enhance the directive's behavior.

For example, let's create a custom directive v-focus that sets the focus on an input element when it's initially rendered:

javascriptCopy code

```
// Register a global custom directive called `v-focus`
Vue.directive('focus', { // bind function bind(el, binding) { // Check if the directive has a modifier named 'delay' if (binding.modifiers.delay) { setTimeout(() => { el.focus(); }, 100); } else { el.focus(); } }, });
```

In this example, the v-focus directive accepts an optional modifier named delay. If the directive is used with the delay modifier (e.g., v-focus.delay), it will set the focus on the element after a 100-millisecond delay. Otherwise, it will set the focus immediately.

Custom directives can be particularly useful for encapsulating complex or reusable behavior. For instance, you can create directives for handling user interactions like dragging and dropping, managing animations, or integrating with third-party libraries. This abstraction not only simplifies your component templates but also makes your code more maintainable and testable.

Additionally, custom directives can be shared across multiple Vue.js projects or even published as open-source packages for the Vue.js community to use. This promotes code reuse and fosters collaboration among developers working on Vue.js applications.

When creating custom directives, it's essential to follow best practices and maintain clarity and consistency in your code. Consider providing clear and concise documentation for your directives, including usage examples and explanations of any available arguments or modifiers. This documentation will make it easier for other developers (including your future self) to understand and use your custom directives effectively.

In summary, creating custom directives in Vue.js is a valuable skill that allows you to extend the capabilities of your Vue components. By encapsulating complex or reusable behavior in custom directives, you can enhance code readability, promote code reuse, and make your Vue.js applications more maintainable. Custom directives empower you to create cleaner and more declarative templates while keeping your JavaScript logic focused and organized.

Chapter 8: Optimizing Performance for High-Traffic Applications

Performance profiling and optimization are essential aspects of software development, as they directly impact the user experience and the efficiency of your applications. Next, we'll explore the importance of performance profiling, various profiling techniques, and optimization strategies to help you build fast and responsive software.

Performance profiling is the process of analyzing your software's execution to identify bottlenecks, resource usage, and areas for improvement. By profiling your application, you gain insights into its behavior, allowing you to pinpoint performance issues and make informed optimization decisions.

Profiling can be applied at various levels of software development, from the high-level architecture of your application down to specific functions or code blocks. Each level of profiling provides valuable information for optimizing your software effectively.

One common way to profile applications is by measuring their execution time. Profiling tools can track how long different parts of your code take to execute, helping you identify performance bottlenecks. Slow functions or code blocks can be identified and optimized to reduce execution time.

Another crucial aspect of performance profiling is memory usage analysis. Profiling tools can monitor memory allocation and deallocation, allowing you to detect memory leaks or inefficient memory usage. Understanding your application's memory usage is vital for preventing crashes and ensuring optimal performance.

Profiling tools often provide detailed reports and visualizations to help you interpret the collected data. These reports can include call graphs, flame graphs, and memory usage charts, making it easier to identify and prioritize optimization opportunities.

One commonly used profiling tool for JavaScript applications is the Chrome DevTools Performance panel. It allows you to record and analyze the runtime performance of your web applications. You can view a timeline of events, inspect function execution times, and identify rendering bottlenecks.

In addition to Chrome DevTools, there are other profiling tools and libraries available for various programming languages and platforms. For example, in Python, you can use the cProfile module to profile code execution, while in C++, tools like Valgrind offer memory profiling capabilities.

When profiling your applications, it's important to consider the specific goals of your optimization efforts. Are you aiming to reduce response times for web requests, improve rendering performance, or optimize memory usage? Clearly defined goals help you focus your profiling efforts and prioritize optimization tasks.

One key principle of optimization is the Pareto principle, often referred to as the "80/20 rule." It suggests that roughly 80% of the performance gains can be achieved by optimizing 20% of the code. Profiling helps you identify that critical 20% so that you can invest your optimization efforts wisely.

Once you've identified performance bottlenecks through profiling, it's time to apply optimization strategies. Optimization can involve various techniques, from algorithmic improvements to code-level optimizations. Here are some common optimization strategies:

Algorithmic Optimization: Start by examining your algorithms and data structures. Optimizing the algorithmic complexity of your code can lead to significant performance improvements. Consider whether you can replace a slow algorithm with a more efficient one or reduce the number of operations required for a task.

Caching: Introduce caching mechanisms to store and retrieve frequently accessed data. Caching can help reduce the load on databases, APIs, or file systems, improving response times. Popular caching solutions include in-memory caches like Redis and browser caching for web applications.

Lazy Loading: Load resources, such as images, scripts, or data, only when they are needed. Lazy loading prevents unnecessary resource loading and reduces initial page load times. For web applications, lazy loading is crucial for optimizing user experience.

Parallelization: Identify tasks that can be executed concurrently and leverage parallelism. Multi-threading or asynchronous programming can help distribute workloads across multiple CPU cores or processes, improving overall throughput.

Database Optimization: Optimize database queries and indexes to reduce query execution times. Ensure that your database schema is designed efficiently and that you use appropriate indexing strategies. Consider denormalization for read-heavy workloads and caching query results where possible.

Memory Management: Implement efficient memory management practices to minimize memory consumption and prevent memory leaks. Release resources when they are no longer needed, use memory pools for object allocation, and be mindful of data structures that can lead to excessive memory usage.

Code Profiling and Refactoring: Continuously profile and refactor your codebase to eliminate bottlenecks and improve code quality. Identify and optimize hotspots in your code that consume a disproportionate amount of resources.

Minification and Compression: Minify and compress your code and assets to reduce file sizes. Smaller files load faster, which is crucial for web applications. Use tools like UglifyJS and gzip compression to achieve this.

Browser Performance: Optimize client-side performance by reducing the number of network requests, leveraging browser caching, and using asynchronous loading for scripts. Prioritize critical rendering paths to ensure that the most important content is displayed quickly.

Content Delivery: Use Content Delivery Networks (CDNs) to deliver static assets closer to the user. CDNs distribute content across multiple servers worldwide, reducing latency and improving load times for users in different regions.

Testing and Benchmarking: Continuously test and benchmark your application after each optimization step. Performance regression testing ensures that optimizations don't introduce new issues. Benchmarking helps you measure the impact of optimizations accurately.

Profiling in Production: Consider profiling your application in a production environment to capture real-world performance data. Production profiling helps you address issues specific to your deployment environment and user traffic patterns.

Browser DevTools: Utilize browser developer tools to analyze runtime performance in web applications. Chrome DevTools, Firefox Developer Tools, and other browser tools offer profiling capabilities for web development.

Content Delivery Optimization: Optimize the delivery of assets such as images, scripts, and styles by using efficient formats and compression techniques. Leverage modern image formats like WebP, enable HTTP/2 or HTTP/3 for faster asset delivery, and leverage browser cache for static resources.

Monitoring and Alerts: Implement monitoring and alerting systems to proactively identify performance issues in production. Tools like New Relic, Datadog, or custom solutions can help you monitor application health and respond to performance anomalies. Remember that optimization is an iterative process, and it's crucial to measure the impact of each optimization step. Performance profiling tools and monitoring systems are essential for tracking the results of your optimization efforts and ensuring that your application remains performant over time. In summary, performance profiling and optimization are critical for delivering fast and responsive software. By understanding the importance of profiling, leveraging profiling tools, and applying optimization strategies, you can create efficient and enjoyable user experiences in your applications. Regularly profiling and optimizing your software ensures that it continues to meet the demands of your users and remains competitive in today's fast-paced digital landscape.

Caching and load balancing are essential techniques for optimizing the performance, availability, and scalability of web applications. Next, we will delve into the concepts of caching and load balancing, explore their significance in modern web architecture, and discuss various strategies to implement them effectively.

Caching is the process of storing frequently accessed data in a temporary storage location, such as memory or disk, to accelerate subsequent retrievals. Caching can significantly improve application performance by reducing the time and resources required to fetch data from the original source.

Caches are particularly beneficial for data that is expensive to compute or retrieve, such as database queries, API responses, or rendered HTML pages. By storing the results of these operations in a cache, subsequent requests can be served much faster, resulting in reduced latency and improved response times.

There are different types of caching, including:

Content Caching: Storing static content like images, stylesheets, and JavaScript files in a cache to minimize network requests and reduce load times for web pages.

Data Caching: Caching the results of database queries or API responses to avoid repeated querying of the same data.

Page Caching: Storing entire HTML pages or fragments to serve cached content instead of generating dynamic pages for each request.

Object Caching: Caching individual objects or data structures, such as objects in a programming language's memory.

CDN Caching: Utilizing Content Delivery Networks (CDNs) to cache and distribute content globally, reducing latency for users in different regions.

To implement caching effectively, you need to consider cache expiration policies, cache validation mechanisms, and cache eviction strategies. Cache expiration policies determine how long cached data remains valid before it needs to be refreshed from the source. Cache validation mechanisms help ensure that cached data is still accurate and up-to-date. Cache eviction strategies decide which items are removed from the cache when it reaches its capacity limit.

Load balancing, on the other hand, is the process of distributing incoming network traffic across multiple servers or resources. Load balancers are typically deployed in front of a group of servers to evenly distribute requests, prevent overloading of individual servers, and enhance the availability and reliability of an application.

Load balancing is essential for achieving high availability and fault tolerance in web applications. By distributing traffic across multiple servers, load balancers can ensure that if one server becomes unavailable due to hardware failure or other issues, the remaining servers can still handle incoming requests.

Load balancing can be implemented at different layers of the network stack, including:

Network Layer Load Balancing: Distributing traffic based on IP addresses and ports. Network layer load balancers are often used for TCP and UDP-based protocols.

Transport Layer Load Balancing: Balancing traffic at the transport layer (e.g., HTTP/HTTPS) using features like round-robin or weighted distribution. This is common in web applications.

Application Layer Load Balancing: Operating at the application layer by inspecting and routing traffic based on application-specific characteristics. Application layer load balancers can perform content-based routing and are suitable for complex applications.

Load balancers can be hardware appliances or software solutions, with software load balancers gaining popularity due to their flexibility and scalability. Popular load balancing software includes Nginx, HAProxy, and cloud-based solutions like Amazon Elastic Load Balancing (ELB) and Google Cloud Load Balancing.

Now, let's explore some strategies and best practices for effective caching and load balancing:

Caching Strategies:

Cache Invalidation: Implement mechanisms to invalidate or refresh cached data when it becomes stale. This can be triggered by changes to the underlying data source or through a time-based expiration policy.

Cache Busting: Use cache-busting techniques for static assets like CSS and JavaScript by appending a unique version or timestamp to the file URLs. This ensures that clients always fetch the latest version of these assets.

Content Delivery Networks (CDNs): Leverage CDNs to cache and distribute static content globally. CDNs have edge servers in various regions, reducing the latency for users worldwide.

Client-Side Caching: Utilize browser caching headers to instruct clients to cache resources like images, stylesheets, and scripts. Properly configured browser caching can significantly reduce load times for returning users.

Load Balancing Strategies:

Round Robin: A simple load balancing strategy that evenly distributes requests in a circular order to each server in the pool. It's easy to implement but may not consider server health or load.

Weighted Distribution: Assign different weights to servers based on their capacity and performance. Servers with higher weights receive more requests, ensuring efficient resource utilization.

Session Affinity (Sticky Sessions): Route a client's requests to the same server for the duration of their session to maintain session state. This is essential for applications that rely on server-side sessions.

Health Checks: Regularly monitor the health of backend servers by sending health check requests. Unhealthy servers are automatically removed from the pool, preventing them from receiving traffic.

Content-Based Routing: Use load balancers that can inspect request content and route traffic based on specific criteria, such as URL paths or headers. This is useful for microservices architectures.

Global Load Balancing: For geographically distributed applications, employ global load balancers that direct users to the nearest data center or server location.

Failover and Redundancy: Implement redundancy and failover mechanisms to ensure high availability. This includes standby load balancers and backup data centers.

Dynamic Scaling: Integrate load balancing with auto-scaling solutions that automatically adjust the number of backend servers based on traffic and demand.

Caching and load balancing are not mutually exclusive but complementary techniques that work together to optimize web application performance. By effectively caching data and distributing traffic across a pool of servers, you can achieve higher performance, scalability, and availability for your applications. These techniques are fundamental building blocks for modern web architecture and are crucial for delivering responsive and reliable user experiences.

Authentication and authorization are critical aspects of security in any software system, and they play a fundamental role in protecting user data and controlling access to resources. Next, we will explore best practices for implementing authentication and authorization effectively, ensuring that your application remains secure and user data remains protected.

Authentication is the process of verifying the identity of users, ensuring that they are who they claim to be. It is the first line of defense against unauthorized access and malicious users. To implement authentication securely, consider the following best practices:

Use Secure Authentication Methods: Always use strong and secure authentication methods, such as password hashing or multi-factor authentication (MFA). Avoid storing plain text passwords and opt for established password hashing algorithms like bcrypt or Argon2.

Implement Multi-Factor Authentication (MFA): Encourage or require users to enable MFA for their accounts. MFA adds an additional layer of security by requiring users to provide more than one piece of evidence to prove their identity.

Session Management: Implement secure session management to ensure that user sessions are properly authenticated and protected against session fixation attacks. Use secure cookies with appropriate settings, like HttpOnly and Secure flags.

Implement Account Lockout Policies: Implement account lockout mechanisms to prevent brute-force attacks. Lockout accounts temporarily after a certain number of failed login attempts.

User Registration Verification: Require email verification or other forms of confirmation during user registration to ensure that the provided email addresses are valid and controlled by the user.

Password Reset Security: Implement secure password reset mechanisms that require users to confirm their identity through a secure channel (e.g., email) before resetting their passwords.

Rate Limiting: Implement rate limiting to protect against password guessing attacks and other forms of abuse. Limit the number of login attempts within a specified time frame.

User Education: Educate users about password security and best practices. Encourage them to use strong, unique passwords and avoid password reuse.

Authorization, on the other hand, is the process of determining what actions and resources users are allowed to access. Effective authorization mechanisms are crucial for ensuring that users can only perform actions that they are permitted to perform. Here are best practices for implementing authorization:

Role-Based Access Control (RBAC): Use RBAC to define roles and permissions within your application. Assign users to roles, and grant each role the appropriate permissions. Avoid implementing overly complex access control lists (ACLs) that can be hard to manage.

Principle of Least Privilege (PoLP): Follow the principle of least privilege when assigning permissions to users or roles. Only grant the minimum level of access required for users to perform their tasks.

Resource-Based Authorization: Implement resource-based authorization to control access to specific resources (e.g., files, database records). Ensure that users can only access resources they own or are explicitly allowed to access.

Attribute-Based Access Control (ABAC): Consider ABAC for more fine-grained access control based on user attributes (e.g., age, department, location) in addition to roles. ABAC can be useful for complex access scenarios.

Centralized Authorization Logic: Centralize your authorization logic in one place to ensure consistency and maintainability. Avoid duplicating authorization checks throughout your codebase.

Use Frameworks and Libraries: Leverage existing authentication and authorization frameworks and libraries. Building your own security mechanisms from scratch can lead to vulnerabilities.

API Security: For APIs and microservices, implement proper authentication and authorization mechanisms, such as OAuth 2.0 or JWT (JSON Web Tokens). Ensure that API endpoints are protected and accessible only to authorized clients.

Audit Trails: Implement audit trails and logging for authorization decisions. Keep records of who accessed what resources and when, which can be crucial for security investigations and compliance.

Regular Security Audits: Conduct regular security audits and code reviews to identify and fix potential authorization vulnerabilities. Engage security experts or penetration testers to assess your application's security posture.

Error Handling: Implement secure error handling for unauthorized access attempts. Avoid exposing sensitive information in error messages that could aid attackers.

Deny by Default: Adopt a "deny by default" approach in your authorization logic. Only grant access if a user or role has explicit permission to access a resource or perform an action.

Testing and Validation: Thoroughly test your authorization mechanisms to ensure they work as intended. Test both positive scenarios (authorized access) and negative scenarios (unauthorized access).

Regular Updates: Stay informed about security vulnerabilities and updates related to the authentication and authorization components you use. Keep your dependencies and libraries up to date to address security issues promptly.

Security Training: Provide security training to development and operations teams to raise awareness of best practices and potential risks.

Incident Response Plan: Develop an incident response plan to handle security incidents, including unauthorized access or data breaches. Define procedures for communication, investigation, and mitigation.

Remember that security is an ongoing process, and threats evolve over time. Regularly review and update your authentication and authorization mechanisms to address emerging security challenges and protect your application and user data effectively.

In summary, authentication and authorization are vital components of application security. By following best practices in these areas, you can safeguard user accounts, control access to resources, and build a robust defense against unauthorized access and security threats. Stay vigilant, keep up with security trends, and continuously assess and improve your authentication and authorization strategies to maintain a secure and trusted application.

BOOK 4
JAVASCRIPT NINJA
HARNESSING THE FULL POWER OF THE LANGUAGE

ROB BOTWRIGHT

Chapter 1: Becoming a JavaScript Ninja: Mastering the Mindset

Designing a full-stack architecture is a complex but crucial task for building modern web applications that deliver rich user experiences. Next, we will explore the various components and considerations involved in designing a full-stack architecture that meets the requirements of your application and supports scalability, maintainability, and performance.

The full-stack architecture encompasses both the frontend and backend components of an application, providing a holistic view of how the system operates. To design an effective full-stack architecture, you should begin by defining the architectural goals and requirements of your application.

Consider the following key aspects when designing your full-stack architecture:

User Experience: Start by understanding the user experience requirements of your application. Identify the target audience, user personas, and the types of devices and platforms your application needs to support. This information will guide your frontend design choices, such as the user interface (UI) and user experience (UX) design.

Scalability: Determine the scalability requirements of your application. Consider factors like expected user growth, peak usage periods, and the ability to scale both horizontally (adding more servers) and vertically (upgrading server capacity). Scalability planning is critical to ensure your application can handle increased loads.

Data Modeling: Define the data model for your application, including the structure of databases, data storage, and data relationships. Choose an appropriate database management system (DBMS) based on the nature of your data and the required performance characteristics.

API Design: Plan the design of your application's APIs (Application Programming Interfaces) that enable communication between the frontend and backend. Determine the API endpoints, data formats (e.g., JSON, XML), and authentication mechanisms.

Security: Prioritize security considerations in your architecture. Implement security measures such as encryption, authentication, authorization, input validation, and protection against common web application vulnerabilities (e.g., SQL injection, cross-site scripting).

Microservices vs. Monolith: Decide whether your architecture will be monolithic, where all components are tightly integrated, or microservices-based, where various components are decoupled and run as separate services. Microservices offer scalability and flexibility but require careful management.

Technology Stack: Select the technologies and frameworks that best align with your project's requirements. Consider factors like programming languages, frontend frameworks (e.g., React, Angular, Vue.js), backend frameworks (e.g., Express.js, Django,

Ruby on Rails), and deployment options (e.g., cloud providers, containers).

Database Management: Choose the appropriate database systems, including relational databases (e.g., MySQL, PostgreSQL), NoSQL databases (e.g., MongoDB, Cassandra), or a combination based on specific data storage needs.

State Management: Determine how your application will manage client-side and server-side state. For frontend state, consider using state management libraries like Redux or Vuex. For server-side state, design session management and caching strategies.

Communication: Plan how different components of your architecture will communicate. This includes frontend components communicating with each other, the frontend communicating with the backend, and microservices (if used) interacting with one another.

Testing and Quality Assurance: Define a strategy for testing your application, including unit testing, integration testing, and end-to-end testing. Establish continuous integration and continuous deployment (CI/CD) pipelines for automated testing and deployment.

Monitoring and Logging: Implement monitoring and logging solutions to track the performance, availability, and health of your application. Use tools like application performance monitoring (APM) and log aggregation services to gain insights into issues and bottlenecks.

Deployment and Scaling: Create deployment strategies and scaling plans. Decide how you will deploy your application (e.g., cloud-based, on-premises, containers) and how you will handle auto-scaling during traffic spikes.

Error Handling and Recovery: Design robust error handling and recovery mechanisms. Consider how your application will handle and recover from errors gracefully to minimize disruptions to users.

Documentation: Maintain thorough documentation for your architecture, including API documentation, database schema documentation, and architecture diagrams. Documentation is crucial for onboarding new team members and troubleshooting issues.

Compliance and Regulations: Ensure that your architecture complies with relevant regulations and data protection laws, such as GDPR or HIPAA. Implement privacy and security measures to protect user data.

Backup and Disaster Recovery: Establish backup and disaster recovery plans to safeguard data and ensure business continuity in case of unexpected events.

Performance Optimization: Continuously monitor and optimize the performance of your architecture. Identify and address performance bottlenecks to deliver a smooth user experience.

Feedback Loop: Create a feedback loop for gathering input from users and stakeholders. Regularly assess the effectiveness of your architecture and make improvements based on feedback.

Team Collaboration: Foster collaboration between frontend and backend development teams. Effective communication and collaboration are essential for aligning the two sides of the stack.

Designing a full-stack architecture is an iterative process that involves making informed decisions based on your application's unique requirements. Regularly review and refine your architecture as your application evolves and grows. Remember that the architecture should be flexible enough to accommodate changes and adapt to emerging technologies and user needs.

By following these best practices and considering the key aspects outlined above, you can create a robust and well-structured full-stack architecture that supports the long-term success of your web application.

Chapter 2: Advanced JavaScript Fundamentals Revisited

The journey to JavaScript mastery is an exciting and rewarding one, filled with opportunities to learn and grow as a developer. JavaScript, as one of the most widely used programming languages in the world, offers a vast landscape of possibilities for those willing to embark on this journey. Whether you are a complete beginner or an experienced developer looking to deepen your JavaScript knowledge, this roadmap will guide you through the key milestones and learning paths to reach JavaScript mastery.

At the very beginning of your journey, as a beginner, you'll start by understanding the fundamentals of JavaScript. This includes grasping the core concepts of variables, data types, operators, and basic control structures. You'll learn how to write your first JavaScript programs, exploring the language's syntax and structure.

As you progress, it's essential to delve into more advanced topics like functions and scope. Functions are the building blocks of JavaScript, and understanding how to create and use them effectively is crucial. You'll explore concepts like function parameters, return values, and closures, which allow you to encapsulate data and behavior.

Once you have a solid grasp of the basics, you'll dive into working with arrays and objects. These data structures are fundamental in JavaScript, and mastering them is essential. You'll learn how to manipulate arrays using methods like map, filter, and reduce, and you'll discover how objects and their properties work.

Next, you'll venture into the world of the Document Object Model (DOM). Understanding the DOM is crucial for web development, as it allows you to interact with and manipulate web page elements using JavaScript. You'll learn how to select and modify DOM elements, handle events, and create interactive web applications.

With a strong foundation in frontend development, you'll explore asynchronous programming with promises and async/await. This is a critical skill for handling tasks like making API requests and managing asynchronous code execution. You'll learn how to write clean and efficient asynchronous code while avoiding callback hell.

As you advance further, you'll explore more complex topics like object-oriented programming (OOP) in JavaScript. You'll understand how to create and work with classes and prototypes, enabling you to build maintainable and scalable applications.

With a solid understanding of the language itself, you'll start exploring popular JavaScript frameworks and libraries. These tools can significantly boost your productivity and open up new possibilities for building web applications. Frameworks like React, Angular, and Vue.js are worth exploring, depending on your project requirements and personal preferences.

During your journey, don't forget the importance of good coding practices and debugging skills. Learning how to write clean, readable, and maintainable code is essential for collaborating with other developers and ensuring the long-term success of your projects. Debugging skills will help you identify and fix issues efficiently, saving you time and frustration.

As you continue to learn, consider exploring advanced JavaScript topics like closures, prototypal inheritance, and functional programming. These concepts will deepen your understanding of the language and make you a more versatile developer.

One key aspect of JavaScript mastery is staying up-to-date with the latest developments in the JavaScript ecosystem. The language evolves rapidly, with new features and updates regularly introduced. Stay connected with the developer community through blogs, forums, and conferences to keep your skills sharp.

In your journey to JavaScript mastery, building projects is essential. Hands-on experience allows you to apply what you've learned, reinforce your knowledge, and gain confidence as a developer. Start with small projects and gradually take on more complex challenges. Consider creating a personal portfolio website, a to-do list application, or a simple game to showcase your skills.

Collaboration with others is another crucial aspect of your journey. Working on team projects and contributing to open-source projects can provide valuable insights and help you learn from experienced developers. Sharing your knowledge and helping others in the community can also enhance your skills and reputation.

Throughout your journey, remember that it's perfectly normal to encounter challenges and roadblocks. Programming can be challenging, but each obstacle you overcome makes you a better developer. Don't be discouraged by errors or difficulties; view them as opportunities to learn and grow.

As you approach JavaScript mastery, consider specializing in areas that align with your interests and career goals. For example, you might focus on frontend development, backend development, mobile app development, or even full-stack development. Specialization allows you to dive deeper into specific technologies and become an expert in your chosen field.

To solidify your expertise, consider pursuing certifications or formal education in web development and JavaScript. Certifications from recognized organizations can validate your skills and open up new career opportunities. Additionally, pursuing a bachelor's or master's degree in computer science or a related field can provide a comprehensive understanding of programming principles.

As you reach the pinnacle of JavaScript mastery, remember that learning is a lifelong journey. Technology constantly evolves, and there will always be new challenges and opportunities to explore. Stay curious, keep pushing your boundaries, and embrace the joy of continuous learning.

In summary, the journey to JavaScript mastery is an exciting and fulfilling adventure. Starting with the fundamentals and gradually progressing to advanced topics, you'll acquire the knowledge and skills needed to excel as a JavaScript developer. Stay persistent, practice regularly, collaborate with others, and never stop seeking new challenges. JavaScript mastery is not just about becoming a skilled programmer; it's about becoming a creative problem solver and a valuable member of the global developer community.

In the world of programming, data is at the heart of everything we do, and understanding advanced data types and objects is a fundamental aspect of mastering JavaScript. Next, we will explore the intricacies of these concepts, delving into arrays, objects, functions, and other data structures that enable us to represent and manipulate complex information in our code.

Let's start with arrays, which are one of the most commonly used data structures in JavaScript. An array is a collection of values, organized in a linear fashion, with each value accessible via an index. What makes arrays powerful is their ability to store a mix of different data types, including numbers, strings, objects, and even other arrays.

Creating an array in JavaScript is as simple as enclosing a list of values in square brackets, like this: [1, 2, 3, 4, 5]. You can access individual elements in an array using square brackets and an index, such as myArray[0] to retrieve the first element. Remember that JavaScript arrays are zero-indexed, so the first element is at index 0.

Arrays come with a rich set of methods and operations that make them versatile and useful. For instance, you can add elements to an array using the push method, remove elements with pop, or manipulate elements using methods like map, filter, and reduce. These methods allow you to perform complex operations on arrays with minimal code.

One important concept to understand when working with arrays is mutability. Arrays in JavaScript are mutable, meaning you can change their content by adding, removing, or modifying elements. This can be both a benefit and a potential source of bugs, so it's crucial to be mindful of how you manipulate arrays.

Next, let's explore objects, another fundamental data type in JavaScript. Objects are collections of key-value pairs, where each key is a string (or a symbol in modern JavaScript) and each value can be of any data type. Objects are often used to represent real-world entities or structures in code, making them versatile and powerful.

You can create an object by enclosing key-value pairs in curly braces, like this: { name: "John", age: 30 }. To access values in an object, you use dot notation or bracket notation. For example, person.name or person["name"] would both retrieve the value "John" from the object person.

Objects in JavaScript can have methods, which are simply functions defined as values of object properties. These methods allow objects to encapsulate behavior, making them more than just data containers. For example, you can have an object representing a car with methods like startEngine and stopEngine.

One important characteristic of objects in JavaScript is that they are reference types. This means that when you assign an object to a variable or pass it as an argument to a function, you're working with a reference to the object in memory, not a copy of it. Understanding reference types is crucial for avoiding unexpected behavior when working with objects.

Another advanced data type worth exploring is functions. In JavaScript, functions are first-class citizens, which means they can be treated as data, assigned to variables, and passed as arguments to other functions. This capability makes functions incredibly powerful and flexible.

You can define functions using the function keyword or, in modern JavaScript, using arrow functions () => {}. Functions can take parameters, which act as placeholders for values that the function will use when called. These parameters can have default values, making functions more robust and versatile.

Functions can also return values using the return statement. This allows you to encapsulate logic and calculations within functions, making your code more modular and easier to understand. Additionally, JavaScript supports anonymous functions, which are functions without a name, often used for one-time operations or as arguments to other functions.

Closures are a concept closely related to functions in JavaScript. A closure is a function that "closes over" its lexical environment, meaning it retains access to the variables and values from its surrounding scope, even after that scope has finished executing. Closures are powerful because they enable data encapsulation and private variables in JavaScript.

Understanding the this keyword in JavaScript is essential when working with objects and functions. this refers to the current execution context and can change depending on how a function is called. Arrow functions, introduced in ES6, have a lexical this, which means they inherit the this value from their enclosing scope. Regular functions, on the other hand, have a dynamic this, which can be influenced by how they are called.

Advanced data types and objects also include concepts like classes and prototypes, which are essential for building complex applications. In modern JavaScript, you can use classes to create blueprints for objects, defining their structure and behavior. Classes provide a more structured way to create objects with shared properties and methods.

Prototypes, on the other hand, are an underlying mechanism in JavaScript that allows objects to inherit properties and methods from other objects. Understanding prototypes is crucial for comprehending how inheritance works in JavaScript. You can access an object's prototype using the __proto__ property or, more commonly, using the Object.getPrototypeOf() method.

Inheritance in JavaScript is prototype-based, which means objects can inherit properties and methods from other objects via their prototypes. This concept is different from classical inheritance found in some other programming languages. In JavaScript, you can create a chain of objects that inherit from each other, allowing you to build complex structures and relationships.

When it comes to working with data, it's essential to consider data validation and manipulation. JavaScript provides various built-in methods and techniques for validating data types, parsing data, and formatting data for display or storage. Regular expressions, or regex, are a powerful tool for pattern matching and data validation in strings.

Another advanced data type to explore is the Set object, introduced in ES6. A Set is a collection of unique values, which can be of any data type. Sets are handy for tasks that require storing and managing a list of distinct items, such as removing duplicates from an array or checking for the presence of specific values.

Maps are another ES6 addition to JavaScript's data types. A Map is a collection of key-value pairs, similar to objects, but with some key differences. Unlike objects, Map keys can be of any data type, and the order of key-value pairs is preserved. Maps are useful for scenarios where you need to maintain the order of elements or use non-string keys.

As you delve into advanced data types and objects, consider the importance of data immutability and functional programming concepts. Immutability, which means that data cannot be changed once it's created, is a core concept in functional programming. It leads to more predictable and maintainable code, especially when working with complex data structures.

Functional programming concepts, such as pure functions, higher-order functions, and immutability, can greatly enhance your ability to work with advanced data types and objects effectively. These concepts promote modularity, reusability, and testability in your code.

In summary, mastering advanced data types and objects in JavaScript is essential for becoming a proficient developer. These concepts form the foundation of your ability to represent, manipulate, and work with data effectively. By understanding arrays, objects, functions, closures, classes, prototypes, and other advanced data types, you'll have the tools you need to build sophisticated applications and solve complex problems with JavaScript.

Chapter 3: Functional Programming in JavaScript

In the world of modern JavaScript development, functional programming concepts are gaining significant attention and importance. One of the key ideas within functional programming is the concept of pure functions, which are at the heart of writing robust and predictable code. Pure functions play a crucial role in achieving code that is easier to reason about, test, and maintain.

At its core, a pure function is a function that always produces the same output for the same input and has no side effects. This means that given a specific set of arguments, a pure function will consistently return the same result, without modifying any external state or variables. The result of a pure function depends solely on its input parameters, making its behavior predictable and reliable.

In contrast, impure functions are functions that can produce different results for the same input or have side effects. Side effects can include modifying global variables, altering the state of objects, or performing I/O operations like reading from or writing to files or databases. Impure functions are more challenging to reason about and can lead to unexpected behavior and bugs in your code.

Pure functions have several advantages that make them valuable in functional programming and JavaScript development. First and foremost, their predictability and lack of side effects make them excellent candidates for testing. When you test a pure function, you can be confident that its behavior won't change unexpectedly, making your tests more reliable and easier to maintain.

Pure functions also promote code modularity and reusability. Since they rely only on their input parameters, you can use them in various parts of your codebase without worrying about unintended consequences. This encourages a clean separation of concerns and a more organized code structure.

Additionally, pure functions are inherently thread-safe and parallelizable. In multi-threaded or concurrent environments, having functions that don't rely on shared state can prevent race conditions and synchronization issues. This property is particularly valuable when working with JavaScript in contexts like Node.js, where concurrency and parallelism can be essential.

To illustrate the concept of pure functions, consider a simple example:

javascriptCopy code

```javascript
function add (a, b) { return a + b; }
```

The add function is pure because it takes two arguments, a and b, and returns their sum without modifying any external variables or state. No matter how many times you call add(2, 3), it will always return 5.

On the other hand, an impure version of the add function might look like this:

javascriptCopy code

```
let result = 0; function impureAdd(a) { result += a;
return result; }
```
In this case, the impureAdd function modifies the external result variable, making it impure. Calling impureAdd(2) multiple times will produce different results and alter the state of the result variable with each call.

To embrace pure functions in your JavaScript code, strive to minimize side effects and mutable state. Avoid modifying global variables, objects, or arrays within your functions. Instead, aim to create functions that take inputs and return outputs without altering external state.

Immutability is another fundamental concept closely related to pure functions in functional programming. Immutable data structures are those that cannot be changed after they are created. In JavaScript, some data types, like strings and numbers, are naturally immutable because you cannot change their values in place. However, objects and arrays are mutable by default, meaning you can modify their properties or elements after creation.

To achieve immutability with objects and arrays, you can follow a few practices:

Avoid Mutating Operations: Instead of using methods like push, pop, splice, or directly modifying object properties, prefer methods that create new data structures, such as concat, slice, map, and filter.

Use the Spread Operator: The spread operator (...) allows you to create copies of objects and arrays with additional or modified properties.

Immutable Libraries: Consider using libraries like Immutable.js or Immer that provide immutable data structures and utilities for working with them.

Here's an example of using immutability to update an array without modifying the original:

javascriptCopy code

```javascript
const originalArray = [1, 2, 3]; const newArray = [...originalArray, 4]; // originalArray is still [1, 2, 3], while newArray is [1, 2, 3, 4]
```

Similarly, you can achieve immutability with objects:

javascriptCopy code

```javascript
const originalObject = { name: "John", age: 30 }; const newObject = { ...originalObject, age: 31 }; // originalObject is { name: "John", age: 30 }, and newObject is { name: "John", age: 31 }
```

Immutability ensures that once you create a data structure, it remains constant, making it easier to reason about and test your code. It also helps prevent subtle bugs that can arise from unexpected mutations.

In functional programming, the use of pure functions and immutability fosters a functional style of programming, where you focus on transforming data rather than modifying it. This style encourages the creation of small, reusable functions that take inputs, perform transformations, and produce outputs without side effects.

To embrace these concepts fully, you can explore libraries and tools that promote functional programming in JavaScript, such as Ramda, Lodash/fp, or Redux for state management in frontend applications. These libraries provide utilities and patterns that align with functional principles and can help you write more maintainable and predictable code. In summary, understanding and applying functional programming concepts like pure functions and immutability can significantly improve the quality and reliability of your JavaScript code. By favoring pure functions and immutable data structures, you can write code that is easier to test, reason about, and maintain. Functional programming principles are valuable not only for building robust applications but also for enhancing your overall programming skills and problem-solving abilities in JavaScript and beyond.

Chapter 4: Metaprogramming and Reflection

In the realm of functional programming, higher-order functions are a pivotal concept that empowers developers to write cleaner, more concise, and modular code. A higher-order function is, in essence, a function that either takes one or more functions as arguments or returns a function as its result, or both. This concept allows for powerful and flexible abstractions, enabling you to build complex behavior from simple, reusable components.

Higher-order functions are prevalent in JavaScript and are essential to understanding the language's functional capabilities. They provide a means to manipulate functions as first-class citizens, enabling you to treat functions just like any other data type. In doing so, you can pass functions as arguments to other functions, return functions from functions, and store functions in variables or data structures.

One common use case for higher-order functions is the process of transforming data. Mapping, filtering, and reducing are fundamental higher-order functions that operate on arrays or collections of data. These functions allow you to apply a given operation or function to each element of an array, selectively filter elements based on a condition, or aggregate data into a single value.

For instance, the map function applies a specified transformation function to each element of an array and returns a new array containing the transformed values. Here's an example:

```
javascriptCopy code
const numbers = [1, 2, 3, 4, 5]; const doubled =
numbers.map((number) => number * 2); // doubled is
now [2, 4, 6, 8, 10]
```

In this case, the map function takes an anonymous function that doubles each number in the numbers array.

Filtering, on the other hand, allows you to create a new array containing only the elements that satisfy a particular condition.

```
javascriptCopy code
const numbers = [1, 2, 3, 4, 5]; const evenNumbers
= numbers.filter((number) => number % 2 === 0); //
evenNumbers is now [2, 4]
```

The filter function takes a function that returns true for elements that should be included in the new array.

The reduce function is another powerful higher-order function that combines elements of an array into a single value, often used for aggregation or summarization.

```
javascriptCopy code
const numbers = [1, 2, 3, 4, 5]; const sum =
numbers.reduce((accumulator, currentValue) =>
accumulator + currentValue, 0); // sum is now 15
```

In this example, the reduce function takes an anonymous function that accumulates the sum of the elements in the numbers array.

Higher-order functions promote code reusability and modularity by encapsulating specific behaviors in functions that can be applied to various data sets. You can easily swap out the transformation, filtering, or aggregation logic by providing different functions to these higher-order functions.

Functional composition is another critical concept that arises from the use of higher-order functions. It involves combining multiple functions to create a new function that performs a sequence of operations. Functional composition enables you to build complex behaviors by composing simpler, reusable functions together.

Consider a scenario where you need to apply a series of transformations to a piece of data. Instead of writing a monolithic function that contains all the logic, you can break it down into smaller, composable functions. Then, you can compose these functions to achieve the desired result.

For example, let's say you have a string that needs to be converted to uppercase, trimmed, and then split into an array of words. You can create three separate functions for each of these tasks:

javascriptCopy code

```javascript
const toUpperCase = (str) => str.toUpperCase(); const
trim = (str) => str.trim(); const splitIntoWords = (str)
=> str.split('');
```

Now, you can use a higher-order function like compose to create a new function that combines these three functions into a single operation:

javascriptCopy code

```javascript
const compose = (...functions) => (input) =>
functions.reduceRight((output, func) => func(output),
input); const processString = compose(splitIntoWords,
```

251

trim, toUpperCase); const originalString = ' Hello, World '; const result = processString(originalString); // result is now ['HELLO,', 'WORLD']

In this example, the compose function takes an array of functions and returns a new function that applies each function in reverse order, from right to left.

Functional composition is not limited to chaining functions sequentially. You can also use it to build more complex behaviors by combining functions in different ways. For instance, you can use the compose function to create a new function that first splits a string into words and then counts the number of words:

javascriptCopy code

```
const countWords = compose((arr) => arr.length, splitIntoWords); const originalString = 'This is a sample sentence'; const wordCount = countWords(originalString); // wordCount is now 5
```

This demonstrates the versatility of functional composition and how it allows you to build functions that perform sophisticated operations while maintaining readability and modularity.

Another concept related to functional composition is currying, which involves transforming a function that takes multiple arguments into a sequence of functions, each taking a single argument. Currying allows you to partially apply a function by providing some of its arguments upfront, resulting in a new function that takes the remaining arguments.

Here's a simple example of currying:

javascriptCopy code

```
const add = (a) => (b) => a + b; const add5 = add(5);
// create a new function that adds 5 to its argument
const result = add5(3); // result is 8
```

Currying can be especially useful when working with higher-order functions and functional composition, as it allows you to create functions that are more flexible and customizable.

In summary, higher-order functions and functional composition are foundational concepts in functional programming and JavaScript development. They empower you to write more maintainable, modular, and reusable code by encapsulating behavior in functions and composing them to create complex operations. Understanding and applying these concepts will enhance your ability to work with data transformations, code abstractions, and functional paradigms in JavaScript and other programming languages.

Chapter 5: Concurrency and Parallelism with Web Workers

Metaprogramming is a fascinating and advanced concept in the world of programming, offering developers the ability to write code that can modify or generate other code dynamically. It's a powerful tool that can be used to create more flexible and efficient programs, but it also comes with its own set of challenges and considerations.

One of the fundamental aspects of metaprogramming is the ability to inspect and manipulate the structure of programs at runtime. This means that you can write code that can examine the structure of classes, objects, functions, and even modules, and make decisions or modifications based on that structure. A common use case for metaprogramming in JavaScript is modifying object prototypes. In JavaScript, almost everything is an object, and objects can have prototypes that define their properties and behaviors. You can use metaprogramming techniques to add or modify methods and properties of an object's prototype, affecting all instances of that object.

For example, consider a simple JavaScript class representing a person:

javascriptCopy code

```javascript
class Person { constructor(name) { this.name = name; }
sayHello() { console.log(`Hello, my name is ${this.name}`); } }
```

With metaprogramming, you can dynamically add new methods to the Person class's prototype:

javascriptCopy code

```
Person.prototype.sayGoodbye    =    function() {
console.log(`Goodbye, my name is ${this.name}`); };
```
Now, all instances of the Person class have access to the sayGoodbye method, even though it was added after the class was defined. Another powerful aspect of metaprogramming is code generation, which involves creating new code at runtime. This can be particularly useful when you need to generate repetitive code or dynamically configure code based on specific requirements. Template literals, introduced in ES6, provide a convenient way to generate code dynamically. For example, you can use template literals to create SQL queries with dynamic parameters:

javascriptCopy code

```
function createSqlQuery(table, fields) { return `SELECT ${fields.join(', ')} FROM ${table}`; } const query = createSqlQuery('users', ['id', 'name', 'email']); console.log(query); // Output: SELECT id, name, email FROM users
```

Another metaprogramming technique involves using the Function constructor to dynamically create functions. This constructor takes a series of arguments representing function parameters and function body as strings and returns a new function.

Here's an example of using the Function constructor to create a dynamic function:

javascriptCopy code

```
const dynamicFunction = new Function('a', 'b', 'return a + b'); console.log(dynamicFunction(2, 3)); // Output: 5
```

While this technique can be powerful, it's essential to use it with caution, as it can introduce security risks, especially when dealing with user-generated code.

One of the most powerful and widely used metaprogramming features in JavaScript is the ability to work with object reflection. Object reflection allows you to inspect the properties and methods of objects at runtime, which can be valuable for tasks like serialization, data validation, or dynamically adapting to changes in object structure.

In JavaScript, you can use the Object.keys(), Object.values(), and Object.entries() methods to extract information about an object's properties and values. For instance, you can create a function that serializes an object into a query string:

```javascript
javascriptCopy code
function serializeObject(obj) { const keyValuePairs = Object.entries(obj); const queryString = keyValuePairs.map(([key, value]) => `${key}=${value}`).join('&'); return queryString; } const user = { id: 1, name: 'John', email: 'john@example.com' }; const queryString = serializeObject(user); console.log(queryString); // Output: id=1&name=John&email=john@example.com
```

Another useful metaprogramming technique in JavaScript involves the use of decorators. Decorators are functions that can be applied to classes, methods, or properties to modify or enhance their behavior. They are commonly used in frameworks like Angular and libraries like MobX to add functionality such as logging, validation, or memoization to classes and methods.

Here's an example of a simple method decorator that logs the execution of a method:

javascriptCopy code

```
function logExecution(target, key, descriptor) { const
originalMethod = descriptor.value; descriptor.value =
function (...args) { console.log(`Calling ${key} with
arguments: ${args.join(', ')}`); const result =
originalMethod.apply(this, args); console.log(`${key}
returned: ${result}`); return result; }; return descriptor; }
class Calculator { @logExecution add(a, b) { return a +
b; } } const calculator = new Calculator(); const result =
calculator.add(2, 3); // Output: // Calling add with
arguments: 2, 3 // add returned: 5
```

Decorators provide a way to extend and modify the behavior of classes and methods without directly altering their code. While metaprogramming can be a powerful tool, it's essential to use it judiciously and with caution. Metaprogramming can make code more complex and harder to understand, so it's crucial to strike a balance between flexibility and maintainability. When using metaprogramming techniques, consider documenting your code thoroughly and following best practices to ensure its readability and maintainability. In summary, metaprogramming in JavaScript offers developers the ability to inspect, modify, and generate code dynamically, providing greater flexibility and extensibility. By leveraging features like object reflection, code generation, decorators, and more, you can create more efficient and adaptable programs. However, it's crucial to use metaprogramming judiciously and follow best practices to maintain code clarity and avoid potential pitfalls.

Chapter 6: Advanced Asynchronous Patterns: Generators and Async Generators

Web Workers are a crucial part of modern web development, offering the ability to run JavaScript code in the background, separate from the main browser thread. This separation of tasks allows for enhanced performance, improved responsiveness, and a smoother user experience in web applications.

In the early days of web development, JavaScript execution happened in a single thread within the browser. While this worked for simple tasks, it posed limitations when dealing with complex computations, time-consuming operations, or tasks requiring continuous user interaction.

Web Workers were introduced to address these limitations by enabling concurrent execution of JavaScript code. With Web Workers, you can create separate threads for specific tasks, freeing up the main thread to handle user interface interactions without slowdowns.

One of the primary benefits of using Web Workers is improved responsiveness. Since tasks running in Web Workers don't block the main thread, user interactions like clicking buttons or scrolling remain smooth and uninterrupted. This is especially important for applications that involve heavy computations, such as data processing or image manipulation.

Web Workers also provide a solution to the problem of time-consuming operations. Tasks that might take a long time to complete, like parsing large datasets, can be offloaded to a Web Worker, ensuring that the main thread remains available for other essential tasks.

Another advantage of Web Workers is their ability to utilize multiple CPU cores. In today's multi-core processors, Web Workers can take full advantage of the available resources, making parallel processing more efficient and speeding up tasks that can be divided into smaller parts.

Web Workers are not limited to a single type of task; they can handle a variety of operations, from calculations to data manipulation and network requests. This versatility makes them a valuable tool for a wide range of web applications.

Creating a Web Worker is straightforward. You typically define a separate JavaScript file that contains the code to be executed in the worker. Then, you create an instance of the worker and pass the URL of the JavaScript file to its constructor. The worker can send and receive messages from the main thread, allowing for communication between the two.

For example, here's how you can create a simple Web Worker that calculates the factorial of a number:

javascriptCopy code

```
// worker.js self.addEventListener('message', (event)
=> { const number = event.data; const result =
calculateFactorial(number); self.postMessage(result);
```

```
}); function calculateFactorial(n) { if (n <= 1) { return
1; } return n * calculateFactorial(n - 1); }
```

In the main thread:

javascriptCopy code

```
const worker = new Worker('worker.js');
worker.addEventListener('message', (event) => {
const result = event.data; console.log(`Factorial
result: ${result}`); }); const numberToCalculate = 5;
worker.postMessage(numberToCalculate);
```

Web Workers can also be terminated and restarted as needed, allowing you to manage resources efficiently.

Another benefit of Web Workers is enhanced security. Since Web Workers run in a separate thread, they don't have direct access to the DOM or the global scope of the main thread. This isolation minimizes the risk of malicious code compromising the user's experience or accessing sensitive information.

Web Workers are not limited to the browser environment. They can also be used in other contexts, such as server-side JavaScript with technologies like Node.js. This versatility allows for code reuse and consistency across different parts of your application.

In addition to the standard Web Workers, there are specialized types like Shared Workers and Service Workers. Shared Workers can be accessed by multiple windows or tabs of the same web application, enabling shared data and communication between them. Service Workers, on the other hand, are designed to intercept and manage network requests, providing features like offline support and background synchronization.

One common use case for Web Workers is parallelizing data processing. For instance, if you have a web application that performs complex data transformations or computations on large datasets, you can divide the work among multiple Web Workers to take full advantage of the available CPU cores. This results in faster execution and a more responsive user interface.

Another practical application of Web Workers is in web-based games and simulations. Games often require real-time physics calculations, pathfinding, or AI simulations. Using Web Workers, you can distribute these tasks across multiple threads, ensuring that the game runs smoothly without impacting user interactions.

Web Workers can also be beneficial in web applications that involve heavy I/O operations, such as file uploads or downloads. By delegating these tasks to a Web Worker, you can prevent the main thread from becoming unresponsive during lengthy file operations.

Furthermore, Web Workers are valuable for handling background tasks like periodic data updates, notifications, or geolocation tracking. These tasks can be offloaded to a separate thread, allowing the main thread to focus on rendering the user interface and responding to user interactions.

It's important to note that while Web Workers offer many benefits, they also come with some considerations. Communication between the main thread and workers is asynchronous and message-based. This means you'll need to manage data serialization and deserialization when sending and receiving messages. Additionally, not all JavaScript features are available within Web Workers. For example, Web Workers don't have access to the DOM, the window object, or some browser-specific APIs.

In summary, Web Workers are a valuable tool in modern web development, offering benefits such as improved performance, enhanced responsiveness, and the ability to utilize multiple CPU cores. They enable web developers to offload time-consuming and computationally intensive tasks to separate threads, ensuring a smooth user experience. By understanding how to create and use Web Workers effectively, you can take full advantage of their capabilities and enhance the performance of your web applications.

Generators are a powerful and versatile feature introduced in ES6 (ECMAScript 2015) that can fundamentally change the way you handle control flow in JavaScript. They provide a new way to work with asynchronous code, simplify iteration, and even offer a form of cooperative multitasking. To understand the power of generators, it's essential to grasp their underlying concepts and how they can be used effectively in your code.

At its core, a generator is a special type of function in JavaScript. What sets generators apart is their ability to pause execution and then resume it from where it left off. This feature allows you to write asynchronous code that looks and behaves more like synchronous code, making your code more readable and maintainable.

To create a generator function, you use the function* syntax. Inside a generator function, you can use the yield keyword to pause execution and return a value. Here's a simple example of a generator function that yields values:

javascriptCopy code

```
function* simpleGenerator() { yield 1; yield 2; yield
3; } const generator = simpleGenerator();
console.log(generator.next()); // { value: 1, done: false
} console.log(generator.next()); // { value: 2, done:
false } console.log(generator.next()); // { value: 3,
done: false } console.log(generator.next()); // { value:
undefined, done: true }
```

In this example, the generator function simpleGenerator yields three values. Each time the next() method is called on the generator object, it returns an object with a value property containing the yielded value and a done property indicating whether the generator has finished.

Generators are particularly useful for handling asynchronous code in a more readable manner. You can use them in combination with Promises to simplify complex asynchronous workflows. Here's an example of using a generator to control asynchronous tasks:

javascriptCopy code

```
function delay(ms) { return new Promise(resolve =>
setTimeout(resolve, ms)); } function* asyncTask() {
console.log('Start');          yield          delay(1000);
console.log('1 second later'); yield delay(2000);
console.log('3 seconds later'); } async function
runAsyncTask() { const generator = asyncTask(); for
```

await (const _ of generator) { // Using a for-await-of loop to iterate through the generator } } runAsyncTask();

In this example, the asyncTask generator function uses yield to pause execution during asynchronous delays. The for await...of loop is used to iterate through the generator, waiting for each asynchronous task to complete before moving on. This results in a clean and linear way to express asynchronous control flow.

One of the most significant benefits of generators is their ability to implement cooperative multitasking, often referred to as "coroutines." Coroutines allow you to create functions that can yield control back to the caller temporarily, allowing other code to execute before resuming. This feature can be beneficial for managing complex, non-blocking I/O operations.

Here's a simplified example of cooperative multitasking using generators:

javascriptCopy code

```
function* taskA() { console.log('Task A: Start'); yield;
// Pause and yield control console.log('Task A:
Resumed'); yield; // Pause again console.log('Task A:
Completed'); } function* taskB() { console.log('Task B:
Start'); yield; // Pause and yield control
console.log('Task B: Resumed'); yield; // Pause again
console.log('Task B: Completed'); } const generatorA =
taskA(); const generatorB = taskB();
generatorA.next(); // Task A: Start generatorB.next();
// Task B: Start generatorA.next(); // Task A: Resumed
```

```
generatorB.next();      //      Task      B:      Resumed
generatorA.next();      //      Task      A:      Completed
generatorB.next(); // Task B: Completed
```

In this example, taskA and taskB are generators that can yield control back and forth. By calling next() on each generator, you can alternate between executing code in a cooperative manner. This can be especially useful when dealing with tasks that require interleaved execution, such as managing multiple network requests or animations.

Generators are also instrumental in creating custom iterators. You can use them to define how an object should be iterated, allowing you to control the iteration process. This is particularly useful when working with data structures or objects that have complex or non-standard iteration behavior.

For instance, you can define a custom iterator for a tree data structure:

javascriptCopy code

```
class TreeNode { constructor(value) { this.value =
value; this.children = []; } *[Symbol.iterator]() { yield
this.value; for (const child of this.children) { yield *
child; // Recursively yield values from children } } }
const       root       =       new       TreeNode(1);
root.children.push(new                TreeNode(2));
root.children[0].children.push(new    TreeNode(3));
for (const value of root) { console.log(value); }
```

In this example, the TreeNode class defines a custom iterator using a generator. It yields the values of the node and its children recursively, allowing you to iterate through the tree in a depth-first manner.

While generators provide powerful capabilities for controlling control flow and creating custom iterators, they also come with some considerations. One important aspect to keep in mind is that generators are stateful. Calling a generator function multiple times creates new generator objects with their own internal state. This means you can't reuse a generator after it has completed.

Additionally, using generators with Promises or asynchronous code requires careful handling of errors and exceptions. Errors that occur inside a generator are not automatically propagated to the caller; you need to handle them explicitly.

In summary, generators are a versatile and powerful feature in JavaScript that can revolutionize how you manage control flow, handle asynchronous code, and create custom iterators. Their ability to pause and resume execution makes asynchronous code more readable and maintainable. Generators also enable cooperative multitasking and offer a clean way to define custom iteration behavior for objects. By mastering generators, you can take your JavaScript coding skills to the next level and write more elegant and efficient code.

Chapter 7: Memory Management and Performance Optimization

JavaScript memory management is a critical aspect of web development, and it plays a significant role in the performance and stability of your applications. Next, we will delve into the fundamentals of memory management in JavaScript, exploring how the language handles memory allocation, deallocation, and garbage collection.

At its core, memory management is the process of allocating and deallocating memory to store and manage data. In languages like JavaScript, which is dynamically typed and garbage-collected, memory management is handled automatically by the runtime environment. This means that developers don't need to explicitly allocate or deallocate memory as they would in lower-level languages like C or C++.

In JavaScript, memory is allocated to store data in the form of variables, objects, and other data structures. When you create a variable or an object, the JavaScript engine sets aside memory to hold its value or properties. Memory allocation is a dynamic process, and the engine decides when and how much memory to allocate based on the needs of your code.

One of the primary challenges in memory management is dealing with memory leaks. A memory leak occurs when a program unintentionally retains references to objects that are no longer needed, preventing the garbage collector from reclaiming their memory. Over time, these leaks can lead to increased memory consumption and decreased application performance.

To understand memory leaks in JavaScript, it's essential to grasp how the language manages references. JavaScript uses a concept called "reference counting" to keep track of references to objects. Every time a reference to an object is created or copied, the reference count of that object is incremented. Conversely, when a reference is deleted or goes out of scope, the reference count is decremented.

When an object's reference count drops to zero, it means that there are no more references to that object, and it becomes a candidate for garbage collection. The garbage collector is responsible for identifying and reclaiming memory occupied by objects with zero reference counts. JavaScript engines implement various garbage collection algorithms to manage memory efficiently.

One common cause of memory leaks in JavaScript is "circular references." A circular reference occurs when two or more objects reference each other in a way that prevents their reference counts from reaching zero. For example, if object A has a property that references object B, and object B has a property that references object A, a circular reference is formed. Even if there are no external references to these objects, their reference counts will never drop to zero, and they won't be collected by the garbage collector.

To avoid circular references and memory leaks, it's crucial to be mindful of object lifecycles and to explicitly remove references when they are no longer needed. One common practice is to use the null value to break references to objects, allowing them to be collected during the next garbage collection cycle.

Another aspect of memory management in JavaScript is the concept of "garbage collection cycles." Garbage collection is not an instantaneous process; it occurs in cycles or phases. During these cycles, the garbage collector identifies objects with zero reference counts and reclaims their memory. The frequency and efficiency of garbage collection can vary between JavaScript engines.

Modern JavaScript engines use advanced garbage collection algorithms, such as generational garbage collection. These algorithms divide objects into different generations based on their age. Newly created objects belong to the "young generation," and objects that survive multiple garbage collection cycles are promoted to the "old generation." This division allows the garbage collector to focus on collecting short-lived objects more frequently, reducing the impact on application performance.

In addition to automatic garbage collection, JavaScript provides tools for manual memory management, primarily through the use of the delete operator. The delete operator allows you to remove a property from an object, potentially reducing its reference count and making it eligible for garbage collection. However, it's important to note that using delete on variables or global objects doesn't directly free memory; it merely removes references to values, which may eventually lead to memory being reclaimed during a garbage collection cycle.

Memory management becomes especially critical when dealing with large-scale web applications or long-running processes. In these cases, it's essential to be aware of memory usage and potential memory leaks. Memory profiling tools provided by modern web browsers can help identify memory-related issues in your JavaScript code. These tools allow you to monitor memory consumption, detect memory leaks, and analyze memory snapshots to pinpoint problematic areas in your application.

In summary, JavaScript memory management is a vital aspect of web development that impacts the performance and stability of your applications. JavaScript engines automatically handle memory allocation and garbage collection, but developers need to be mindful of potential memory leaks, circular references, and object lifecycles. Understanding how memory management works in JavaScript and using memory profiling tools can help you create efficient and reliable web applications.

Profiling and optimizing JavaScript performance is a crucial aspect of web development, as it directly impacts the user experience and the efficiency of your web applications. Next, we will explore the process of profiling and optimizing JavaScript code, focusing on techniques and tools to identify and address performance bottlenecks.

Performance optimization is a multifaceted process that involves improving the speed and responsiveness of your JavaScript applications. It encompasses various aspects, including reducing execution time, optimizing memory usage, and enhancing the overall user experience. To begin the optimization journey, it's essential to start with profiling—the process of measuring and analyzing code execution to identify performance issues.

JavaScript profilers are tools that help developers gain insights into how their code runs, which functions consume the most time, and where memory is allocated. By profiling your code, you can pinpoint areas that need optimization and make informed decisions on how to improve performance. Several JavaScript profiling techniques and tools are available to aid in this process.

One commonly used JavaScript profiler is the browser's built-in developer tools. Modern web browsers provide comprehensive debugging and profiling tools that can be accessed through the browser's developer console. These tools offer features like CPU profiling, memory profiling, and timeline recording, allowing you to analyze and visualize the performance of your web applications.

CPU profiling is a technique used to measure the amount of CPU time consumed by various functions in your JavaScript code. Profiling tools record function execution times and create call graphs to illustrate the flow of your program. By examining these graphs, you can identify functions that consume significant CPU resources and may require optimization.

Memory profiling, on the other hand, focuses on analyzing memory usage and identifying memory leaks. Memory profilers track the allocation and deallocation of memory in your application. They can help you detect objects that are not properly released, leading to increased memory consumption and potential performance degradation.

To perform memory profiling, you can use browser developer tools to take heap snapshots, which capture the current state of the JavaScript heap at specific points in time. Comparing multiple heap snapshots can reveal objects that are growing in size or accumulating over time, indicating potential memory leaks.

Timeline recording is another valuable feature of browser developer tools. It records a timeline of events, including JavaScript execution, rendering, network activity, and user interactions. Analyzing the timeline can help you understand how various activities in your application affect its overall performance.

In addition to browser-based tools, there are third-party profiling libraries and tools available for JavaScript developers. One such tool is "Chrome DevTools" by Google, which provides a comprehensive set of profiling and debugging features. Another popular choice is "Node.js Inspector," which allows you to profile Node.js applications running on the server-side.

Once you've identified performance bottlenecks through profiling, the next step is to optimize your JavaScript code. Optimization strategies can vary depending on the specific issues you've uncovered, but some general techniques can improve overall performance.

One fundamental optimization technique is code refactoring. Refactoring involves restructuring your code to make it more efficient, readable, and maintainable. By eliminating redundant code, simplifying complex algorithms, and improving data structures, you can often achieve substantial performance gains.

Another key aspect of optimization is minimizing unnecessary work. This can be achieved by reducing the number of function calls, avoiding repetitive calculations, and optimizing loops. For example, caching computed values can prevent redundant calculations and speed up code execution.

In some cases, choosing the right data structure or algorithm can significantly impact performance. Data structures like maps and sets offer fast lookup times, while algorithms like binary search can drastically reduce the time complexity of certain operations. Selecting the appropriate data structure and algorithm for a specific task is essential for optimizing code.

Asynchronous programming is prevalent in JavaScript, especially in web applications. While asynchronous code is essential for non-blocking I/O operations, it can introduce performance challenges. Callback functions and promise chains can become deeply nested, leading to the "callback hell" phenomenon. To address this, consider using async/await, which provides a more readable and structured way to handle asynchronous operations.

Optimizing DOM manipulation is critical for web performance. Frequent updates to the DOM can lead to rendering bottlenecks and slow user interfaces. To mitigate this, use techniques like "batching" DOM updates or leveraging the virtual DOM in libraries like React to minimize unnecessary re-renders.

Reducing network requests and optimizing assets can also improve the performance of web applications. Minimize the size of JavaScript and CSS files by using minification and compression techniques. Utilize browser caching to reduce the number of requests made to the server.

One essential practice in performance optimization is continuous testing and benchmarking. Regularly test your code with profiling tools and measure the impact of optimizations on performance. Benchmarking tools can help you compare the execution times of different code implementations and ensure that your optimizations are effective.

Lastly, consider employing lazy loading and code splitting techniques. Load only the JavaScript that is required for the current page or user interaction. This can significantly reduce initial load times and improve perceived performance.

In summary, profiling and optimizing JavaScript performance are essential steps in creating fast and responsive web applications. Profiling tools, such as browser developer tools, help identify performance bottlenecks by analyzing CPU usage, memory usage, and timeline events. Optimization techniques include code refactoring, minimizing unnecessary work, choosing the right data structures and algorithms, and improving asynchronous code. Regular testing and benchmarking are crucial to ensuring the effectiveness of optimizations. By incorporating these practices into your development workflow, you can deliver a better user experience and make your web applications more efficient and responsive.

Chapter 8: Building Custom JavaScript Libraries

Creating reusable and modular JavaScript code is a fundamental principle of software development that promotes maintainability, scalability, and code efficiency. Next, we will explore the concept of code reusability and modularity in JavaScript, along with best practices for designing and implementing reusable components and modules.

Reusability is a core concept in software engineering, emphasizing the ability to use existing code in different parts of an application or across multiple projects. Reusable code minimizes redundancy, reduces development time, and ensures consistency in functionality and behavior.

JavaScript, as a versatile and widely used programming language, provides various techniques for achieving code reusability. One common approach is creating functions and classes that encapsulate specific functionality, making them easily shareable and reusable.

Functions are a fundamental building block of reusable code in JavaScript. By defining functions that perform specific tasks or operations, you can reuse the same functionality throughout your codebase. For example, a function that calculates the average of an array of numbers can be reused whenever such a calculation is needed.

Parameters and arguments allow you to make functions more versatile. By accepting inputs through parameters, functions can adapt to different use cases. For instance, a sorting function can accept an array and a sorting criterion as parameters, making it reusable for various sorting requirements.

Another way to promote reusability is by using function return values. Functions can return results or values that can be utilized elsewhere in your code. This enables you to create functions that provide specific data or perform calculations and use their results in different parts of your application.

In addition to functions, JavaScript supports the creation of reusable classes. Classes encapsulate data and behavior into objects that can be instantiated multiple times. By defining classes with well-defined properties and methods, you can create reusable components that represent entities, such as users, products, or widgets.

Classes can also inherit from other classes, enabling the creation of class hierarchies. Inheritance allows you to reuse and extend existing classes, inheriting their properties and methods while adding or modifying functionality as needed.

Modularity is closely related to reusability and involves organizing code into smaller, self-contained modules. A module is a unit of code that encapsulates a specific set of functionality or features. Modular code is easier to maintain, test, and reuse, as it promotes separation of concerns and reduces the complexity of individual components.

JavaScript provides several mechanisms for creating and working with modules. One common approach is using the ES6 module system, which allows you to define modules using the export and import keywords. With ES6 modules, you can export functions, classes, or variables from one module and import them into another, making it easy to reuse and share code.

Another widely used module system in JavaScript is CommonJS, commonly used in server-side development with Node.js. CommonJS modules use the module.exports and require statements to define and import modules. While CommonJS is not native to browsers, tools like Webpack and Browserify enable its use in client-side development.

Revealing Module Pattern is a design pattern that provides encapsulation and control over the visibility of functions and variables within a module. By exposing only selected members using the return statement, you can hide implementation details and offer a clean interface for using the module.

Asynchronous Module Definition (AMD) is a module system designed for asynchronous loading of modules in browsers. It is commonly used with libraries like RequireJS to manage dependencies and load modules when needed, improving page load times.

One key advantage of modular code is the ability to manage dependencies effectively. Dependencies are the relationships between different modules, where one module relies on the functionality provided by another. By explicitly defining dependencies, you ensure that modules are loaded in the correct order, preventing runtime errors and promoting a clear structure.

To create truly reusable and modular JavaScript code, follow best practices:

Keep modules small and focused on a specific task or functionality.

Minimize dependencies between modules to reduce coupling.

Use clear and descriptive names for functions, classes, and variables to enhance code readability.

Document the purpose and usage of each module to aid other developers in understanding and using your code.

Test modules independently to verify their correctness and reliability.

Unit testing frameworks like Mocha, Jest, and Jasmine provide tools for testing individual modules and ensuring that they function as expected.

Implement versioning and semantic versioning (SemVer) to manage changes to your modules and communicate compatibility with other code that depends on them.

Consider using package managers like npm (Node Package Manager) or Yarn to distribute and manage modules across projects.

By adhering to these best practices and principles of reusability and modularity, you can create JavaScript code that is not only efficient and maintainable but also easily shareable and adaptable for various applications and contexts.

In summary, creating reusable and modular JavaScript code is a foundational skill for modern web development. It allows you to build efficient, maintainable, and scalable applications by encapsulating functionality into reusable components and organizing code into manageable modules. By embracing reusability and modularity, you can streamline development, reduce errors, and enhance the overall quality of your JavaScript projects.

Documenting and testing your custom JavaScript libraries

is a critical step in ensuring their usability, reliability, and maintainability. Effective documentation and thorough testing help developers understand how to use your libraries, verify their correctness, and identify potential issues.

Documentation serves as a user guide for your library, offering essential information on its purpose, features, and usage. It helps other developers, including yourself, understand how to integrate and leverage your library in their projects.

One common way to provide documentation is by creating a README file for your library's repository. In this file, you can explain the library's functionality, provide usage examples, and detail installation and configuration instructions.

Another popular documentation format is JSDoc comments. JSDoc is a standard for documenting JavaScript code using comments that follow a specific syntax. By adding JSDoc comments to your library's source code, you can generate API documentation automatically.

JSDoc comments include annotations that describe the purpose, parameters, return values, and types of functions and methods. These comments can be processed by documentation generators like JSDoc or tools integrated into code editors, such as Visual Studio Code, to generate documentation in various formats.

When documenting your library, consider including the following information:

A brief introduction to the library, explaining its purpose and benefits.

Installation instructions, including how to install the library using package managers like npm or yarn.

Usage examples, demonstrating how to use the library's functions or classes in various scenarios.

API documentation for each function or method, describing its parameters, return values, and usage guidelines.

Information on configuration options, if applicable, and how to customize the library's behavior.

Code examples and code snippets that illustrate common use cases and best practices.

License information, specifying the terms under which the library can be used and distributed.

Contributions guidelines, encouraging other developers to contribute to the library's improvement.

By providing comprehensive documentation, you empower users to utilize your library effectively and troubleshoot any issues they encounter.

Testing is an essential aspect of library development that ensures its correctness and reliability. Testing involves systematically verifying that your library functions as expected, even when subjected to various inputs and scenarios.

Unit testing is a common testing approach for libraries. Unit tests focus on verifying the correctness of individual functions, methods, or classes in isolation. You can write unit tests that cover different cases, including edge cases and boundary conditions, to ensure robustness.

JavaScript offers various testing frameworks and libraries that facilitate unit testing. Popular choices include Mocha, Jest, Jasmine, and Ava. These frameworks provide a structure for organizing tests, executing them, and reporting results.

In addition to unit tests, you can create integration tests that evaluate how your library interacts with other components or external dependencies. Integration tests help ensure that your library's integration with external systems or libraries works as intended.

Test-driven development (TDD) is a development approach that emphasizes writing tests before implementing functionality. By following TDD, you ensure that your library's code remains testable, and you can catch regressions or errors early in the development process.

Continuous integration (CI) and continuous delivery (CD) pipelines are valuable for automating the testing process. CI/CD systems like Travis CI, CircleCI, and GitHub Actions allow you to run tests automatically whenever changes are pushed to your repository. This ensures that your library's tests are executed consistently, and any issues are detected promptly.

When writing tests, consider the following best practices:

Write clear and descriptive test case names that explain the purpose of each test.

Test both typical and edge cases to cover a wide range of scenarios.

Avoid making tests too brittle by focusing on essential behavior and avoiding implementation details.

Use test runners and assertion libraries that match your development stack and preferences.

Maintain a comprehensive suite of tests to provide confidence in the library's stability.

Code coverage analysis tools can help you identify which parts of your library's code are covered by tests. Code coverage reports show the percentage of code lines, branches, and functions that are executed during testing. Increasing code coverage can help you ensure that your tests thoroughly exercise the library's functionality.

While automated testing is crucial, manual testing can also be valuable for exploring the library's behavior interactively. Manual testing allows you to identify issues that automated tests may miss and gain a better understanding of how users will interact with your library.

Incorporating user feedback is another valuable aspect of testing. By collecting and addressing user-reported issues, you can improve the library's quality and user satisfaction.

In summary, documenting and testing your custom JavaScript libraries are essential practices that contribute to their success and adoption. Effective documentation helps users understand and utilize your library, while testing ensures its correctness and reliability. By following best practices in documentation and testing, you can create libraries that are valuable assets for the development community, fostering collaboration and innovation.

Chapter 9: Server-Side JavaScript with Node.js

Node.js has emerged as a powerful and versatile runtime environment for executing JavaScript code outside of web browsers. Next, we will explore what Node.js is and delve into its various use cases, highlighting the reasons why it has gained widespread popularity in the world of web development and beyond.

Node.js, often simply referred to as Node, is an open-source, cross-platform JavaScript runtime built on Chrome's V8 JavaScript engine. It was created by Ryan Dahl in 2009 and has since become a fundamental tool in the toolkit of many developers.

One of the key features of Node.js is its non-blocking, event-driven architecture, which makes it highly efficient for handling I/O operations and network requests. This design choice enables Node.js to handle a large number of simultaneous connections without significant overhead.

Node.js is particularly well-suited for building server-side applications and services. It can be used to create web servers, APIs, and other networked software. Node.js has a rich ecosystem of libraries and frameworks that simplify the development of server-side applications, with Express.js being one of the most popular choices for building web APIs.

Additionally, Node.js excels at real-time applications, making it an ideal choice for building chat applications, online gaming platforms, and collaboration tools where low latency and high concurrency are essential.

Node.js has also found its place in the world of microservices architecture. Microservices are a software development approach where applications are composed of small, independently deployable services that work together. Node.js's lightweight nature and support for asynchronous operations make it a valuable choice for developing individual microservices that can be orchestrated to create complex systems.

Beyond web development, Node.js has made its mark in the world of desktop applications. Tools like Electron, which is built on Node.js, allow developers to create cross-platform desktop applications using web technologies such as HTML, CSS, and JavaScript. This has led to the development of popular desktop applications like Visual Studio Code, Slack, and Discord.

Node.js has also become a valuable tool in the realm of Internet of Things (IoT) development. Its ability to run on resource-constrained devices and handle real-time communication has made it a popular choice for building IoT applications and devices. Developers can use Node.js to interface with sensors, control hardware, and process data in IoT scenarios.

In the world of cloud computing, Node.js is widely used for serverless computing and function as a service (FaaS) platforms like AWS Lambda and Azure Functions. Serverless architecture allows developers to run code in response to events without managing server infrastructure. Node.js's fast startup times and efficient event handling make it a top choice for serverless applications.

Node.js's package manager, npm (Node Package Manager), is a crucial component of the ecosystem. With npm, developers can easily discover, install, and manage packages and dependencies for their Node.js projects. The npm registry hosts a vast collection of open-source packages, enabling developers to leverage existing code and libraries to accelerate their development process.

The vibrant Node.js community contributes to its continued growth and innovation. Developers from around the world actively maintain and improve Node.js and its ecosystem. Regular updates and new features keep Node.js in sync with the latest JavaScript language enhancements and runtime improvements.

When considering whether to use Node.js for a particular project, it's essential to assess the specific requirements and constraints. Node.js is an excellent choice for applications that require high concurrency, real-time capabilities, or serverless architecture. However, for CPU-intensive tasks that are not well-suited to asynchronous processing, alternative runtimes or languages may be more appropriate.

In summary, Node.js is a powerful and versatile JavaScript runtime that has found its place in a wide range of use cases, from web development and real-time applications to microservices, IoT, desktop applications, and serverless computing. Its non-blocking, event-driven architecture, coupled with a vast ecosystem of packages and libraries, makes it a valuable tool for modern software development. As you explore the world of Node.js, you will discover its capabilities and potential in various domains, empowering you to build efficient and scalable applications across different platforms and industries.

Building RESTful APIs with Express.js is a fundamental skill for web developers who want to create robust and scalable backend services. Next, we will explore the principles and best practices of designing and implementing RESTful APIs using Express.js, a popular web application framework for Node.js.

Representational State Transfer (REST) is an architectural style that defines a set of constraints for creating web services. RESTful APIs adhere to these constraints, making them simple, scalable, and easy to understand. The core principles of REST include stateless communication, client-server architecture, uniform resource identifiers (URIs), stateless requests, and a layered system.

Express.js is a minimalist and flexible Node.js web application framework that simplifies the process of building RESTful APIs. It provides a set of essential features and middleware for handling HTTP requests, routing, and response generation. To get started with Express.js, you need to install it using npm, Node.js's package manager, and create an Express application.

One of the first steps in building a RESTful API with Express.js is defining the routes and endpoints that clients can access. Routes are defined using HTTP methods (such as GET, POST, PUT, DELETE) and associated with specific URIs. Each route corresponds to a specific resource or functionality in the API.

Middleware functions play a crucial role in Express.js, allowing you to add processing logic for requests and responses. Middleware functions can perform tasks like authentication, input validation, logging, and error handling. You can use existing middleware or create custom middleware to suit your API's requirements.

When defining routes, it's essential to follow RESTful conventions for naming and structuring endpoints. For example, a RESTful endpoint to retrieve a list of users could be structured as /api/users using the HTTP GET method. To create a new user, you might use /api/users with the HTTP POST method.

RESTful APIs typically use HTTP status codes to indicate the outcome of requests. Common status codes include 200 for successful responses, 201 for resource creation, 400 for bad requests, and 404 for resource not found. Express.js simplifies setting status codes and sending responses by providing helper methods like res.status() and res.json().

Express.js allows you to organize your code using routers, which are mini Express applications that can be mounted on specific routes. Routers help maintain a clean and modular code structure, especially for large APIs with multiple endpoints. You can create separate router modules for different parts of your API, such as users, products, or orders.

Authentication is a critical aspect of many RESTful APIs, as it ensures that only authorized users can access certain resources or perform specific actions. Express.js provides flexibility in implementing authentication strategies, such as token-based authentication, OAuth, or sessions. Popular authentication middleware libraries like Passport.js can be integrated with Express to simplify the authentication process.

Input validation is essential for ensuring the integrity and security of your API. Express.js offers various middleware libraries like express-validator and joi that enable you to validate request data, such as query parameters, request bodies, and route parameters. Validating input helps prevent security vulnerabilities and improves the overall robustness of your API.

Error handling is another critical aspect of API development. Express.js provides a default error handling mechanism, but you can also implement custom error handling to tailor error responses to your API's needs. Using middleware like next(err) allows you to pass errors to error-handling middleware functions.

Testing is an integral part of building reliable RESTful APIs. Unit testing and integration testing help ensure that your API functions correctly and responds appropriately to various scenarios. Popular testing frameworks like Mocha and Jest can be used in combination with libraries like SuperTest for making HTTP requests and asserting responses.

When designing RESTful APIs, versioning can be a useful strategy to manage changes and ensure backward compatibility. You can version your API by including the version number in the URI, headers, or query parameters. Versioning allows clients to continue using older versions of the API while adapting to newer ones gradually.

Documentation is crucial for helping developers understand how to use your API effectively. Providing clear and comprehensive documentation, including API endpoints, request and response formats, authentication methods, and usage examples, makes your API more accessible and user-friendly. Tools like Swagger and Postman can assist in generating and maintaining API documentation.

Securing your RESTful API is paramount to protect sensitive data and prevent unauthorized access.

Implementing security measures like HTTPS encryption, rate limiting, and proper authentication and authorization mechanisms is essential. Regularly updating dependencies and addressing security vulnerabilities is also critical for maintaining a secure API.

Scalability is an important consideration when building RESTful APIs. Express.js applications can be scaled horizontally by adding more servers or instances to handle increased traffic. Additionally, caching strategies, load balancing, and database optimization can contribute to improved performance and scalability.

Monitoring and analytics tools can provide valuable insights into the usage and performance of your API. Monitoring helps identify bottlenecks, errors, and performance issues, allowing you to optimize your API for better user experience.

In summary, building RESTful APIs with Express.js is a core skill for web developers. By following RESTful principles, adhering to best practices, and leveraging the capabilities of Express.js, you can create robust, secure, and well-documented APIs that serve as the foundation for web and mobile applications. Whether you are building a small internal API or a large-scale public service, mastering Express.js for RESTful API development is an essential skill in the modern web development landscape.

Chapter 10: Scaling and Securing Your JavaScript Applications

Scaling strategies are essential for high-traffic applications to ensure that they can handle increased user demand and deliver a seamless user experience. As an application gains popularity, the load on the server infrastructure can grow exponentially, potentially leading to performance bottlenecks and downtime if not managed effectively.

Vertical scaling, also known as scaling up, involves increasing the capacity of individual servers by adding more resources, such as CPU, RAM, or storage. This approach can be a quick solution to handle increased traffic, but it has limitations in terms of scalability, as there is a practical limit to how much a single server can be upgraded.

Horizontal scaling, on the other hand, involves adding more servers to distribute the load across multiple machines. This approach offers better scalability and redundancy, making it suitable for handling high traffic. Horizontal scaling can be achieved by deploying multiple server instances behind a load balancer, which distributes incoming requests evenly across the servers.

Load balancing plays a crucial role in distributing traffic effectively across multiple servers. Load balancers can be implemented at various levels, including DNS-based load balancing, network load balancing, and application load balancing. Using a load balancer ensures that each server receives a fair share of incoming requests, preventing any single server from becoming a bottleneck.

Caching is an effective strategy for reducing the load on the server infrastructure. Caching involves storing frequently accessed data in memory or on disk so that it can be quickly retrieved without the need to generate it dynamically. Popular caching solutions like Redis and Memcached can be used to speed up database queries and reduce the load on database servers.

Content Delivery Networks (CDNs) are another powerful tool for scaling high-traffic applications. CDNs distribute static assets, such as images, CSS, and JavaScript files, to multiple geographically distributed edge servers. This ensures that content is served from a server closest to the user, reducing latency and improving load times. CDNs also help offload the origin server, reducing its load.

Database scaling is a critical consideration for applications that rely heavily on databases. Vertical scaling of databases involves increasing the resources of a single database server, which can be done by upgrading hardware or moving to a more powerful database instance. Horizontal scaling of databases, also known as sharding, involves partitioning data across multiple database servers. Sharding can be challenging to implement but can significantly improve database performance and scalability.

Microservices architecture is a design approach that involves breaking down an application into smaller, independent services that can be developed, deployed, and scaled separately. Microservices allow teams to work on different parts of an application independently, making it easier to scale individual services as needed. Containerization technologies like Docker and container orchestration platforms like Kubernetes facilitate the deployment and scaling of microservices.

Serverless computing is a cloud computing model where developers write code that runs in response to events without the need to manage server infrastructure. Serverless platforms automatically scale resources up or down based on demand, making it an excellent choice for high-traffic applications with variable workloads. Popular serverless platforms include AWS Lambda, Azure Functions, and Google Cloud Functions.

Auto-scaling, a feature offered by many cloud providers, allows resources to be automatically added or removed based on predefined metrics or triggers. For example, an auto-scaling group in Amazon Web Services (AWS) can be configured to increase the number of virtual machines (EC2 instances) when CPU usage exceeds a certain threshold. Auto-scaling ensures that the application can handle varying levels of traffic efficiently.

Monitoring and performance tuning are ongoing processes that are essential for maintaining the scalability of high-traffic applications. Monitoring tools can provide insights into the application's performance, allowing for proactive adjustments. Performance tuning involves optimizing code, database queries, and server configurations to ensure optimal resource utilization.

Content optimization is another strategy for improving the scalability of high-traffic websites. Reducing the size of web assets, such as images and scripts, can lead to faster page load times and reduced bandwidth usage. Techniques like image compression, minification of JavaScript and CSS files, and lazy loading of images can help optimize content delivery.

Global distribution of servers can further enhance the scalability and performance of high-traffic applications. By deploying servers in multiple regions or data centers, you can reduce latency and improve the user experience for a geographically diverse audience. Content can be served from the nearest server to the user, ensuring minimal delays.

Failover and disaster recovery planning are crucial aspects of scaling strategies. High-traffic applications must be prepared for unexpected server failures or outages. Implementing redundancy and failover mechanisms, such as backup servers and data replication, can help ensure the availability of the application even in the face of hardware or network issues.

Cost management is an essential consideration when scaling high-traffic applications. While cloud services offer scalability, they also come with associated costs. Careful monitoring of resource usage and cost optimization strategies, such as reserved instances or spot instances, can help manage expenses effectively.

In summary, scaling high-traffic applications is a multifaceted process that requires careful planning and the use of various strategies and technologies. Vertical and horizontal scaling, load balancing, caching, CDNs, database scaling, microservices, serverless computing, and auto-scaling are all valuable tools in a developer's toolkit. Regular monitoring, performance tuning, content optimization, global distribution, failover planning, and cost management are essential practices to ensure that high-traffic applications remain responsive and available to users, regardless of the demands placed on them.

Securing Node.js applications is a critical aspect of modern web development, as the popularity of Node.js continues to grow. With its event-driven, non-blocking I/O model, Node.js is well-suited for building fast and scalable web applications, but it also introduces unique security challenges that developers must address.

One fundamental principle of Node.js security is to keep your packages and dependencies up to date. Outdated packages may contain known vulnerabilities that attackers can exploit. By regularly updating your packages and using tools like npm audit to identify and fix security issues, you can reduce your application's exposure to potential threats.

Authentication is a core component of securing web applications. Properly implementing user authentication and authorization ensures that only authenticated and authorized users can access specific resources. Popular authentication libraries like Passport.js can simplify the implementation of authentication strategies such as local username and password, OAuth, and JWT-based authentication.

Session management is crucial for maintaining user state securely. Using secure and random session tokens, implementing session timeouts, and storing session data in a secure way are essential practices. Additionally, using the express-session middleware can help manage user sessions effectively in Express.js applications.

Data validation is a critical step in preventing security vulnerabilities such as SQL injection, Cross-Site Scripting (XSS), and Cross-Site Request Forgery (CSRF). Input data, whether it comes from users or external sources, should be validated and sanitized to ensure it meets expected criteria. Using libraries like express-validator or joi can simplify input validation and help prevent common security flaws.

When dealing with user input or any untrusted data, it's essential to use parameterized queries or prepared statements to prevent SQL injection attacks. Avoid constructing SQL queries using string concatenation and instead rely on libraries that support parameterized queries. Using an Object-Relational Mapping (ORM) like Sequelize or an ODM like Mongoose can also help prevent SQL injection.

Cross-Site Scripting (XSS) attacks occur when untrusted data is included in web pages without proper escaping. To prevent XSS, always sanitize user input and escape data when rendering it in HTML or JavaScript contexts. Frameworks like React provide built-in mechanisms for escaping data when rendering components, reducing the risk of XSS vulnerabilities.

Cross-Site Request Forgery (CSRF) attacks involve tricking users into making unauthorized requests to a web application while they are authenticated. To mitigate CSRF attacks, use anti-CSRF tokens and ensure that sensitive operations, such as changing passwords or deleting accounts, require authentication and authorization. Frameworks like Express.js offer middleware like csurf to help protect against CSRF attacks.

Another crucial security practice is implementing proper access control. Ensure that users can only access resources and perform actions that they are authorized to do. Use role-based access control (RBAC) or attribute-based access control (ABAC) mechanisms to manage permissions effectively.

Input validation should also extend to file uploads. Always validate and limit the types and sizes of files that users can upload to prevent potential security risks such as executable files or large files that could exhaust server resources. Use libraries like multer to handle file uploads securely.

Securely storing sensitive data, such as passwords and API keys, is vital for protecting user information. Never store passwords in plaintext; instead, use cryptographic hashing algorithms like bcrypt to store and verify passwords securely. Store API keys and other secrets in environment variables or use a secure secrets management solution.

Implementing proper logging and monitoring is essential for identifying and responding to security incidents. Log all security-relevant events, such as failed login attempts or access control violations. Use tools like centralized logging solutions and security information and event management (SIEM) systems to analyze and detect unusual patterns or potential security threats.

Regular security audits and code reviews can help identify vulnerabilities and ensure that security best practices are followed. Engage in penetration testing and security assessments to assess the resilience of your application to potential attacks. Consider using automated security testing tools to scan your codebase for common vulnerabilities.

Securing your application's dependencies is crucial, as vulnerabilities in third-party packages can impact your application's security. Regularly update your dependencies and monitor for security advisories related to the packages you use. Use tools like npm audit or package managers like Yarn to check for known vulnerabilities.

Network security is another aspect to consider when securing Node.js applications. Implement firewall rules and security groups to restrict access to your application's servers. Use HTTPS to encrypt data in transit and implement security headers to protect against common web vulnerabilities like clickjacking and cross-site scripting.

Deploying a Web Application Firewall (WAF) can provide an additional layer of protection by filtering and monitoring incoming web traffic for malicious activity. WAFs can help mitigate threats like SQL injection, XSS, and DDoS attacks.

Distributed Denial of Service (DDoS) attacks can disrupt your application's availability. Implementing DDoS mitigation strategies, such as rate limiting, traffic filtering, and using content delivery networks (CDNs), can help protect your application from DDoS attacks.

Containerization and orchestration technologies like Docker and Kubernetes offer security features that can help isolate and secure your application's components. Leverage container security best practices, such as scanning images for vulnerabilities and configuring container runtime security.

Regularly review and update your security policies and procedures to adapt to evolving threats and compliance requirements. Stay informed about the latest security vulnerabilities and best practices by participating in security communities and following security news sources.

In summary, securing Node.js applications requires a comprehensive approach that encompasses authentication, authorization, input validation, secure coding practices, secure data storage, access control, monitoring, and ongoing security assessments. By following best practices and staying vigilant, developers can build and maintain secure Node.js applications that protect user data and ensure the integrity of web services in an increasingly interconnected digital world.

Conclusion

In "JavaScript Bootcamp: From Zero to Hero - Hands-On Learning for Web Developers," we embarked on a transformative journey through the world of JavaScript, equipping ourselves with the knowledge and skills necessary to excel in web development. Across four comprehensive books, we delved into the depths of JavaScript, progressing from novice to ninja in our pursuit of mastery.

In "Book 1 - JavaScript Fundamentals: A Beginner's Guide to Web Development," we laid the foundation for our learning, building a solid understanding of JavaScript's core concepts and syntax. We explored the essential building blocks of the language, such as variables, data types, control flow, functions, and working with arrays and objects. This book provided the necessary groundwork for our journey ahead.

"Book 2 - Intermediate JavaScript Mastery: Building Web Applications with ES6 and Beyond" took our skills to the next level. We delved into the world of ES6 and modern JavaScript, uncovering powerful features and techniques to craft dynamic web applications. We learned about advanced topics like asynchronous programming with Promises, DOM manipulation, and event handling. By the end of this book, we were equipped to build interactive and responsive web applications with confidence.

"Book 3 - Advanced JavaScript Techniques: Mastering Complex Projects and Frameworks" challenged us to push the boundaries of our JavaScript expertise. We delved into complex projects and explored the world of JavaScript frameworks, mastering tools and techniques required for building scalable and maintainable applications. Topics such as React, Angular, and Vue.js allowed us to navigate the intricacies of modern web development with ease.

Finally, in "Book 4 - JavaScript Ninja: Harnessing the Full Power of the Language," we ascended to the ranks of JavaScript ninjas, wielding the language's full potential. We explored advanced concepts such as functional programming, metaprogramming, concurrency, and memory management. Armed with this knowledge, we were ready to tackle even the most challenging development tasks and create custom JavaScript libraries to suit our unique needs.

As we conclude our journey through "JavaScript Bootcamp: From Zero to Hero," we emerge as web development professionals who can confidently navigate the ever-evolving landscape of JavaScript. We have acquired the skills and knowledge to create web applications, solve complex problems, and adapt to emerging technologies. Whether you are a beginner looking to kickstart your web development journey or an experienced developer seeking to refine your skills, this book bundle has equipped you with the tools to succeed.

In the world of web development, JavaScript remains a cornerstone, and our journey through these four books has given us the expertise and confidence to build exceptional web experiences. Remember, the learning doesn't stop here; it's just the beginning of a lifelong journey to harness the limitless possibilities of JavaScript. May your coding adventures be fruitful, your projects innovative, and your career as a JavaScript developer truly heroic.

www.ingramcontent.com/pod-product-compliance
Lightning Source LLC
Chambersburg PA
CBHW071235050326
40690CB00011B/2123